The SPIRIT of AMERICA

The SPIRIT of AMERICA

BOOKCRAFT
Salt Lake City, Utah

Copyright © 1998 by Bookcraft, Inc.

All rights reserved. No part of this book may be reproduced in any form or by any means without permission in writing from the publisher, Bookcraft, Inc., 2405 W. Orton Circle, West Valley City, Utah 84119.

Bookcraft is a registered trademark of Bookcraft, Inc.

Library of Congress Catalog Card Number 98-71541
ISBN 1-57008-423-8

First Printing, 1998

Printed in the United States of America

We are close to the true source and principle of national greatness. It is in the national spirit.... I anticipate the day when to command respect in the remotest regions it will be sufficient to say I am an American.

—Gouverneur Morris

Contents

	Publisher's Preface ix	
1	"Righteousness Exalteth a Nation" . . . . 1 PRESIDENT EZRA TAFT BENSON	
2	The Divinely Inspired Constitution . . . . 11 ELDER DALLIN H. OAKS	
3	America Must Look to God . . . . 29 PRESIDENT GORDON B. HINCKLEY	
4	The Country with a Conscience . . . . 39 ELDER BOYD K. PACKER	
5	Liberty, License, and Law. . . . . 57 ELDER RUSSELL M. NELSON	
6	"First in War, First in Peace, First in the Hearts of His Countrymen". . . . . 69 ELDER L. TOM PERRY	
7	Religion in a Free Society . . . . 81 ELDER M. RUSSELL BALLARD	
8	America: "God Mend Thine Every Flaw". . . . . 93 ELDER NEAL A. MAXWELL	
9	Some Responsibilities of Citizenship . . . . 105 ELDER DALLIN H. OAKS	

10	*The Integrity of Obeying the Law* .... *125* PRESIDENT JAMES E. FAUST	
11	*"Except the Lord Build the House"* .... *137* ELDER JEFFREY R. HOLLAND	
12	*Our Nation's True Source of Strength* .... *151* PRESIDENT GORDON B. HINCKLEY	
	Index *159*	

Publisher's Preface

The first July Fourth celebration in Provo, Utah, was held less than one year after Brigham Young sent a small group of pioneer families to a wild area along the banks of the Provo River. Since that time America's Freedom Festival at Provo has become one of the nation's largest Independence Day celebrations.

The festival's presentations reflect the expression of John Adams, who wrote in 1776 that drafting the Declaration of Independence "will be the most memorable epoch in the history of America. I am apt to believe that it will be celebrated by succeeding generations as the great anniversary festival. It ought to be commemorated as the day of deliverance, by solemn acts of devotion to God Almighty. It ought to be solemnized with pomp and parade, with shows, games, sports, guns, bells, bonfires and illuminations, from one end of the continent to the other from this time forward for evermore."

A prominent feature in the festival is the Patriotic Service, in which thousands of people gather in the BYU Marriott Center to hear an address by a member of either the First Presidency or the Council of the Twelve Apostles of The Church of Jesus Christ of Latter-day Saints. Thousands more meet in other locations to witness the event via satellite broadcast.

By arrangement with the authors and with America's Freedom Festival at Provo, Bookcraft is pleased to be able to make available in book form the twelve addresses delivered in the Patriotic Service in recent years. These leaders speak from both mind and heart as they remind us of our blessings as Americans, and how these may be preserved to our nation—that "if it so be that they shall serve him according to the commandments which he hath given, it shall be a land of liberty unto them."

To complement the talks, the publisher has selected quotations from important figures in American history and placed them on pages opposite chapter openings.

Bookcraft is confident that people of goodwill everywhere will find this book informative and inspiring.

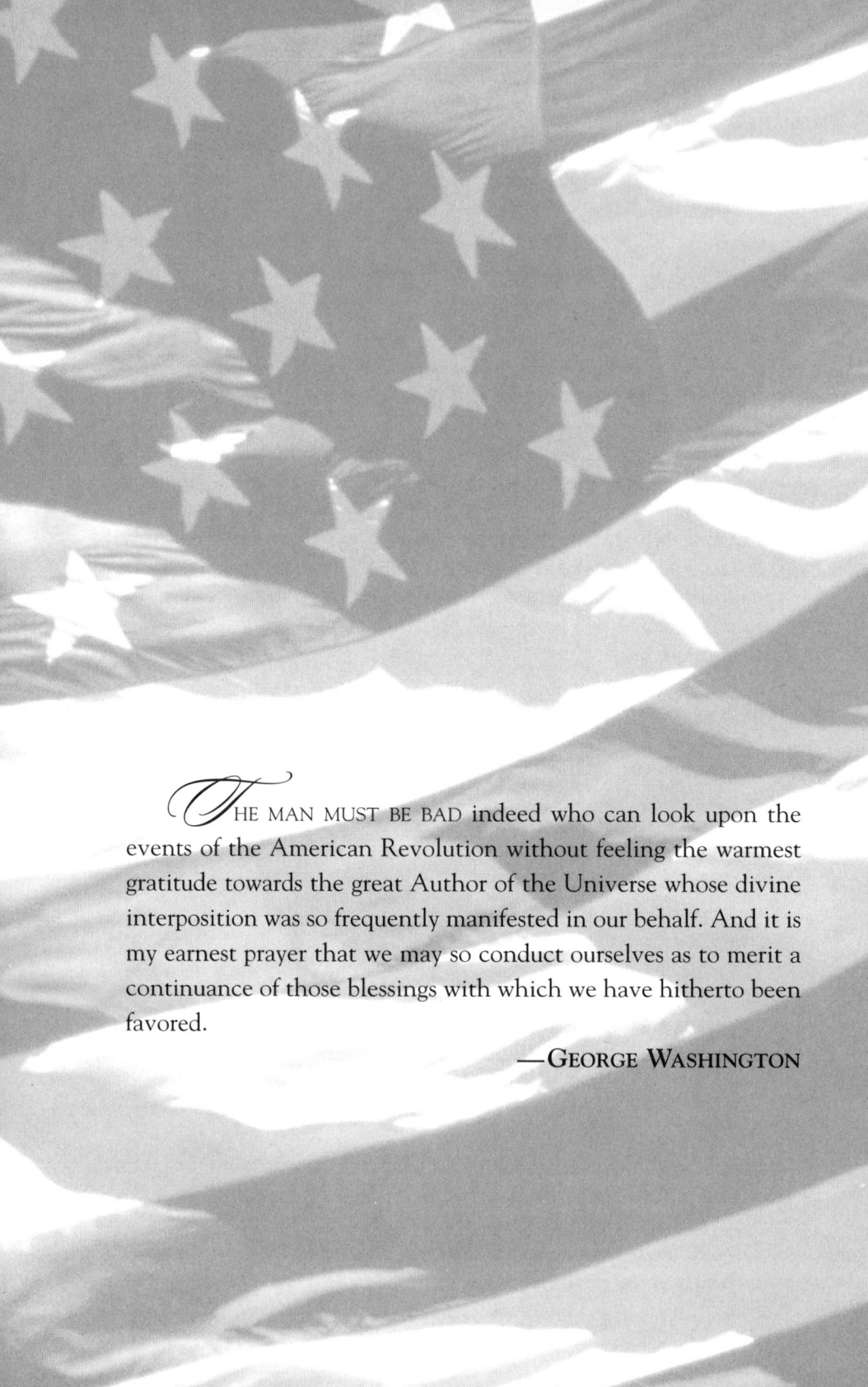

The man must be bad indeed who can look upon the events of the American Revolution without feeling the warmest gratitude towards the great Author of the Universe whose divine interposition was so frequently manifested in our behalf. And it is my earnest prayer that we may so conduct ourselves as to merit a continuance of those blessings with which we have hitherto been favored.

—George Washington

1

"Righteousness Exalteth a Nation"
President Ezra Taft Benson

My fellow Americans, I would like to use as a text for my address this day a verse from the Old Testament: "Righteousness exalteth a nation" (Proverbs 14:34). This is the key to understanding our heritage, and this is the key to maintaining it. The foundations of America are spiritual. That must never be forgotten or doubted. Lest we forget, let us review those beginnings, looking for the spiritual moorings which underpin our nation.

This nation began with the founding of Plymouth Colony in 1620. You are all familiar with the pilgrimage that brought the Puritans to this land.

They had come to these shores under financial sponsorship of the Virginia Company of London and of Plymouth, England. Their intent was to settle in the Virginia Colony but they landed far to the north, where the king of England had no authority. Since England had no government for them, they decided to form a government of their own.

Assembled in the cabin of the *Mayflower*, forty-one adult males formed a compact as the source of their authority. That compact was drafted in "the name of God." Their reasons for a

---

Address given 29 June 1986.

government were also asserted: "For the Glory of God" and "the advancement of the Christian faith." These are the twin pillars of our religious freedom in this nation!

One hundred and two pilgrims had left England for the promised land. Fifty-one, just half the colony, survived the first winter. Not one of the survivors returned to England.

They formed a commonwealth based on the principle of religious liberty—faith in an omnipotent God.

> Ay, call it holy ground,
>   The soil where they first trod,
> They have left unstained what they found—
>   Freedom to worship God.
>   —Felicia Dorothea Hemans

Hardly had the new nation had its beginning than oppression came from the mother country. Injustice, oppressive taxation, the despised Navigation Acts—these led the colonists to deliberate on their rights and liberties under the crown.

A petition to the king failed.

Then the shot heard round the world was fired at Lexington.

A year later, in the summer of 1776, the Continental Congress met in Philadelphia and declared independence from England.

The doctrine of that crowning document—the Declaration of Independence—is this: That the Creator, God, endowed all men with basic rights, and that governments derive their powers from the consent of the governed.

Until the American Revolution, a millennium of political tradition vested powers only in monarchs and dictators. The formers of our republic simply declared the truth—that God gave all men the right to life, liberty, and property. Man, therefore, was master over government rather than the other way around.

That is what the American Revolution was all about—not just a separation from England, but a separation from the historical tradition that made one man another's chattel and denied all men liberty and property.

While some vacillated on whether to separate from England and adopt the Declaration of Independence, the sentiments of John Adams were described by Daniel Webster as follows:

> Sink or swim, live or die, survive or perish, I give my hand and my heart to this vote. It is true, indeed, that in the beginning we aimed not at independence. But there's a divinity which shapes our ends . . . why, then, should we defer the Declaration?
>
> You and I, indeed, may rue it. We may not live to the time when this Declaration shall be made good. . . . but whatever may be our fate, be assured, . . . that this Declaration will stand. It may cost treasure, and it may cost blood: but it will stand, and it will richly compensate for both. . . .
>
> My judgment approves this measure, and my whole heart is in it. All that I have, and all that I am, and all that I hope, in this life, I am now ready here to stake upon it; and I leave off as I began, that live or die, survive or perish, I am for the Declaration. It is my living sentiment, and by the blessing of God it shall be my dying sentiment, independence, now, and independence forever. (*The Works of Daniel Webster*, 4th ed., 1851, 1:133–36.)

From the standpoint of numbers, equipment, training, and resources the rag-tag army of the colonists should never have won the war for independence. But America's destiny was not to be determined by overwhelming numbers, or better military weapons, or strategy. As Adams declared: "There's a divinity which shapes our ends." God took a direct hand in the events that led to the defeat of the British.

When the war was over, here is how Washington ascribed the victory: "The success, which has hitherto attended our united efforts, we owe to the gracious interposition of heaven, and to that interposition let us gratefully ascribe the praise of victory, and the blessings of peace." (To the Executives of New Hampshire, November 3, 1789.)

It seems fashionable today for historians to "secularize" our history. Many modern scholars seem uncomfortable with the idea that a divine power had a hand in the beginnings of our nation. They seek to explain away what the colonists themselves saw as divine intervention in their behalf. They credit even those remarkable events to "natural causes" or "rational" explanations. All events are explained from a "humanistic" frame of reference. This removes the need for faith in God or a belief that He is interested in the affairs of men.

But the founding fathers had no problems with seeing the hand of the Lord in the birth of the nation. As we have noted, George Washington gave direct credit to God for the victory over the British in the Revolutionary War. But that did not end the need for inspiration and divine help.

The newly formed nation was hardly a united commonwealth. At best it could be described as a federation of colonies loosely held together by the Articles of Confederation. Under this instrument the nation had no head—no president, and no supreme court—only a congress devoid of power! In addition, rebellions and potential anarchy threatened the victory won by war.

Providentially, a Constitutional Convention was called in 1787. We celebrate the two hundredth anniversary next year. The delegates met from May 25 to September 17 with George Washington presiding. A central issue was whether they were to merely revise the Articles of Confederation or write a new constitution.

Debates were earnest and at times it appeared that the convention was deadlocked. On one of those occasions, the elder statesman of the group, Benjamin Franklin, appealed to the delegates. He declared:

> I have lived, sir, a long time, and the longer I live, the more convincing proofs I see of this truth, that God governs in the affairs of men. And, if a sparrow cannot fall to the ground without his notice is it probable that an empire can rise without his aid?

> We have been assured, sir, in the sacred writings, that "except the Lord build the house, they labor in vain that build it."
>
> I firmly believe this; and I also believe, that, without his concurring aid, we shall succeed in this political building no better than the builders of Babel; . . .
>
> I therefore beg leave to move, that henceforth prayers, imploring the assistance of heaven, and its blessings on our deliberations, be held in this assembly every morning before we proceed to business: and that one or more of the clergy of this city be requested to officiate in that service. (Jared Sparks, *The Works of Benjamin Franklin*, 1837, pp. 155–56.)

The deadlock was broken. Compromises were made.

A constitution was drafted, and 39 of 55 delegates signed it. Again, I would ask: why is it that the references to God's influence in the noble efforts of the founders of our republic are not mentioned by modern historians? Listen to the convictions of two of these delegates to the Constitutional Convention. First, Charles Pinckney:

> When the great work was done and published, I was . . . struck with amazement. Nothing less than that superintending hand of Providence, that so miraculously carried us through the war . . . , could have brought it about so complete, upon the whole. (P. L. Ford, ed., *Essays on the Constitution*, 1892, p. 412.)

Here is another testimony, this from James Madison, sometimes referred to as the father of the Constitution.

> It is impossible for the man of pious reflection not to perceive in it a finger of that Almighty hand which has been so frequently and signally extended to our relief in the critical stages of the revolution. (*The Federalist*, No. 37.)

The fact that our founding fathers looked to God for help and inspiration should not surprise us, for they were men of great faith. These men had been raised up specifically by the Lord so they could participate in the great political drama unfolding in America. President Wilford Woodruff, while serving as an Apostle and also as president of the St. George Temple, said: "I am going to bear my testimony to this assembly, if I never do it again in my life, that those men who laid the foundation of this American Government . . . were the *best spirits* the God of Heaven could find on the face of the earth. They were choice spirits, *not wicked men*. General Washington and all the men that labored for the purpose were inspired of the Lord." (General Conference address, April 10, 1898.)

Yes, our nation's foundation is spiritual. Without spirituality we are no better than any of the other nations which have sunk into oblivion.

Our founding fathers, with solemn and reverent expression, voiced their allegiance to the sovereignty of God, knowing that they were accountable to Him in the day of judgment. Are we less accountable today? I think not. I urge you to keep the commandments and to pray for our nation and its leaders.

The founding fathers understood that principle "righteousness exalteth a nation" (Proverbs 14:34) and helped to bring about one of the greatest systems ever used to govern men. But unless we continue to seek righteousness and preserve the liberties entrusted to us, we shall lose the blessings of heaven. Thomas Jefferson said, "The price of freedom is eternal vigilance." The price of freedom is also to live in accordance with the commandments of God. The early founding fathers thanked the Lord for His intervention in their behalf. They saw His hand in their victories in battle and believed strongly that He watched over them.

The battles are not over yet, and there will yet be times when this great nation will need the overshadowing help of Deity. Will we as a nation be worthy to call upon Him for help? President Brigham Young said: "We all believe that the Lord will fight our battles; but how? Will he do it while we are unconcerned and make no effort whatever for our own safety when the enemy is upon us? . . . The Lord requires us to be quite as willing to fight our own battles as to have Him fight them for us. If we are not ready for the enemy when he comes upon us, we have not lived up to the requirements of Him who guides the ship of Zion, or who dictates the affairs of the Kingdom." (*Journal of Discourses*, 11:131.)

How do we prepare ourselves so that God will intervene in our behalf in the days ahead? I would like to suggest four important things we can do.

1. *We must, both as individuals and as a nation, look to God as our maker and as the source of our freedoms and blessings.* Our nation has faced many crises since its founding. One of the most grave was the Civil War. Once again the Lord had raised up a great man to be the man of the hour. Abraham Lincoln understood the spiritual foundations of America and the need for divine help and guidance. He called upon the people to have a day of national fasting and prayer. His proclamation contains wisdom and counsel of great worth to us today:

> It is the duty of nations as well as men to own their dependance upon the overruling power of God, to confess their sins and transgressions in humble sorrow, yet with assured hope that genuine repentance will lead to mercy and pardon, and to recognize the sublime truth, announced in the Holy Scriptures and proven by all history, that those nations only are blessed whose God is the Lord. (In John Wesley Hill, *Abraham Lincoln—Man of God* [New York: G. P. Putnam's Sons, 1927], p. 390.)

2. *We must make the creation of quality family life a high priority in our lives.* Families are the foundation blocks of any society. When the majority of families are strong and self-reliant, the nation prospers and dwells safely. But today there are many forces pulling at the fabric of family life. One of the primary goals of The Church of Jesus Christ of Latter-day Saints is to support strong family life.

We teach and emphasize that the key to family stability is happy marriage based on family worship. Divorce is deplored.

We are actively engaged in teaching fathers to be compassionate fathers, and mothers, full-time mothers in the home. Fathers are commanded to take the lead in all spiritual matters. We encourage parents to teach their children fundamental spiritual principles that will instill faith in God, faith in their family, and faith in their country. We plead with parents to spend time with their children, both in teaching them and in building positive relationships. These are the things that create and foster strong family units and a stable society.

3. *We must become informed and knowledgeable citizens.* The Lord said through the prophet Hosea, "My people are destroyed for lack of knowledge" (Hosea 4:6). We must not let that happen here. There are two important things we must do.

A. We must study and learn for ourselves the principles laid down in the Constitution which have preserved our freedoms for the last two hundred years. If we do not understand the role of government and how our rights are protected by the Constitution, we may accept programs or organizations that help erode our freedoms. An informed citizenry is the first line of defense against anarchy and tyranny.

B. We must teach our children about the spiritual roots of this great nation. We must become actively involved in supporting programs and textbooks in the public schools that teach the greatness of the early patriots who helped forge our liberties. We must teach our children that it is part of our faith that the Constitution of the United States was inspired by God. We reverence it akin to the revelations that have come from His hand. The great heritage of freedom bequeathed to us by our forebears must be handed on to each succeeding generation with great care.

4. *We must become actively involved in supporting good, wise, and honest people for public office and assume an active part in improving our communities.* Edmund Burke once said, "The only thing necessary for the triumph of evil is for good men to do nothing" (in John Bartlett, *Familiar Quotations* [Boston: Little, Brown and Co., 1968], p. 454). It is not enough that we wring our hands and moan about conditions in America. We must seek out good men and women and support them in running for public office. We must become involved in programs that seek to stop the decay of

morality in America. We must become responsible citizens and carry out our civic duty. We should be "anxiously engaged" in good causes and leave the world a better place for having lived in it.

My fellow Americans, we live in a great and glorious land. We have been the beneficiaries of great blessings from heaven. We must not ever forget the blessings that have been bestowed upon us. Our nation is still in deep need of the help of the Almighty. We need His inspiration. We need His guidance. We need His protection. When we as a people not only desire to do His will but also determine we will do it, then we can expect that help from our God.

I testify to you that the foundations of our country are spiritual. I testify that God has watched over us and blessed us greatly. I witness to you that those who keep the commandments of God will continue to be blessed in this land, for "righteousness exalteth a nation." God bless us all to be faithful. And may our Heavenly Father bless this land and preserve our divine constitution and the republic which it established, I humbly pray in the name of Jesus Christ, amen.

I CONSENT, SIR, TO THIS Constitution because I expect no better, and because I am not sure that it is not the best.

—BENJAMIN FRANKLIN

2

The Divinely Inspired Constitution

ELDER DALLIN H. OAKS

Not long after I began to teach law, an older professor asked me a challenging question about Latter-day Saints' belief in the United States Constitution. Earlier in his career he had taught at the University of Utah College of Law. There he met many Latter-day Saint law students. "They all seemed to believe that the Constitution was divinely inspired," he said, "but none of them could ever tell me what this meant or how it affected their interpretation of the Constitution." I took that challenge personally, and I have pondered it for many years.

I hope I will not be thought immodest if I claim a special interest in the Constitution. As a lawyer and law professor for more than twenty years, I have studied the United States Constitution. As legal counsel, I helped draft the bill of rights for the Illinois constitutional convention of 1970. And for three and one-half years as a justice of the Utah Supreme Court I had the sworn duty to uphold and interpret the constitution of the state of Utah and the United States. My conclusions draw upon those experiences and upon a lifetime of studying the scriptures and the teachings of the living prophets. My opinions on this subject are personal

---

From an address given 5 July 1987.

and do not represent a statement in behalf of The Church of Jesus Christ of Latter-day Saints.

CREATION AND RATIFICATION

The United States Constitution was the first written constitution in the world. It has served Americans well, enhancing freedom and prosperity during the changed conditions of more than two hundred years. Frequently copied, it has become the United States' most important export. After two centuries, every nation in the world except six have adopted written constitutions,[1] and the U.S. Constitution was a model for all of them. No wonder modern revelation says that God established the U.S. Constitution and that it "should be maintained for the rights and protection of all flesh, according to just and holy principles." (D&C 101:77.)

George Washington was perhaps the first to use the word *miracle* in describing the drafting of the U.S. Constitution. In a 1788 letter to Lafayette, he said: "It appears to me, then, little short of a miracle, that the delegates from so many different states (which states you know are also different from each other in their manners, circumstances and prejudices) should unite in forming a system of national Government, so little liable to well-founded objections."[2]

It was a miracle. Consider the setting.

The thirteen colonies and three and one-half million Americans who had won independence from the British crown a few years earlier were badly divided on many fundamental issues. Some thought the colonies should reaffiliate with the British crown. Among the majority who favored continued independence, the most divisive issue was whether the United States should have a strong central government to replace the weak "league of friendship" established by the Articles of Confederation. Under the Confederation of 1781 there was no executive or judicial authority, and the national Congress had no power to tax or to regulate commerce. The thirteen states retained all their sovereignty, and the national government could do nothing without their approval. The Articles of Confederation could not be amended without the unanimous approval of all the states, and every effort to strengthen this loose confederation had failed.

Congress could not even protect itself. In July 1783 an armed mob of former Revolutionary War soldiers seeking back wages threatened to take Congress hostage at its meeting in Philadelphia. When Pennsylvania declined to provide militia to protect them, the congressmen fled. Thereafter Congress was a laughingstock, wandering from city to city.

Unless America could adopt a central government with sufficient authority to function as a nation, the thirteen states would remain a group of insignificant, feuding little nations united by nothing more than geography and forever vulnerable to the impositions of aggressive foreign powers. No wonder the first purpose stated in the preamble of the new United States Constitution was "to form a more perfect union."

The Constitution had its origin in a resolution by which the relatively powerless Congress called delegates to a convention to discuss amendments to the Articles of Confederation. This convention was promoted by James Madison and Alexander Hamilton, two farsighted young statesmen still in their thirties, who favored a strong national government. They persuaded a reluctant George Washington to attend and then used his influence in a letter-writing campaign to encourage participation by all the states. The convention was held in Philadelphia, whose population of a little over 40,000 made it the largest city in the thirteen states.

As the delegates assembled, there were ominous signs of disunity. It was not until eleven days after the scheduled beginning of the convention that enough states were represented to form a quorum. New Hampshire's delegation arrived more than two months late because the state had not provided them travel money. No delegates ever came from Rhode Island.

Economically and politically, the country was alarmingly weak. The states were in a paralyzing depression. Everyone was in debt. The national treasury was empty. Inflation was rampant. The various currencies were nearly worthless. The trade deficit was staggering. Rebelling against their inclusion in New York State, prominent citizens of Vermont had already entered into negotiations to rejoin the British crown. In the western territory, Kentucky leaders were speaking openly about turning from the union and forming the alliances of the Old World.

Instead of reacting timidly because of disunity and weakness, the delegates boldly ignored the terms of their invitation to amend the Articles of Confederation and instead set out to write an entirely new constitution. They were conscious of their place in history. For millennia the world's people had been ruled by kings or tyrants. Now a group of colonies had won independence from a king, and their representatives had the unique opportunity of establishing a constitutional government Abraham Lincoln would later describe as "of the people, by the people, and for the people."

The delegates faced staggering obstacles. The leaders in the thirteen states were deeply divided on the extent to which the states would cede any power to a national government. If there was to be a strong central government, there were seemingly irresolvable differences on how to allocate the ingredients of national power between large and small states. As to the nature of the national executive, some wanted to copy the British parliamentary system. At least one delegate even favored the adoption of a monarchy. Divisions over slavery could well have prevented any agreement on other issues. There were 600,000 black slaves in the thirteen states, and slavery was essential in the view of some delegates and repulsive to many others.

Deeming secrecy essential to the success of their venture, the delegates spent over three months in secret sessions, faithfully observing their agreement that no one would speak outside the meeting room on the progress of their work. They were fearful that if their debates were reported to the people before the entire document was ready for submission, the opposition would unite to kill the effort before it was born. This type of proceeding would obviously be impossible today. There is irony in the fact that a constitution which protects the people's "right to know" was written under a set of ground rules that its present beneficiaries would not tolerate.

It took the delegates seven weeks of debate to resolve the question of how the large and small states would be represented in the national congress. The Great Compromise provided a senate with equal representation for each state, and a lower house in which representation was apportioned according to the whole population of free persons in the state, plus three-fifths of the slaves. The vote on this pivotal issue was five states in favor and four against; other states did not vote, either because no delegates were present or because their delegation was divided. Upon that fragile base, the delegates went forward to consider other issues, including the nature of the executive and judicial branches, and whether the documents should include a bill of rights.

It is remarkable that the delegates were able to put aside their narrow sectional loyalties to agree on a strong central government. Timely events were persuasive of the need: the delegates' memories of the national humiliation when Congress was chased out of Philadelphia by a mob, the recent challenge of Shays' rebellion against Massachusetts farm foreclosures, and the frightening prospect that northern and western areas would be drawn back into the orbit of European power.

The success of the convention was attributable in large part to the remarkable intelligence, wisdom, and unselfishness of the delegates. As James Madison wrote in the preface to his notes on the Constitutional Convention: "There never was an assembly of men, charged with a great and arduous trust, who were more pure in their motives, or more exclusively or anxiously devoted to the object committed to them."[3] Truly, the U.S. Constitution was established "by the hands of wise men whom [the Lord] raised up unto this very purpose." (D&C 101:80.)

The drafting of the Constitution was only the beginning. By its terms it would not go into effect until ratified by conventions in nine states. But if the nation was to be united and strong, the new Constitution had to be ratified by the key states of Virginia and New York, where the opposition was particularly strong. The extent of opposition coming out of the convention is suggested by the fact that of seventy-four appointed delegates, only fifty-five participated in the convention, and only thirty-nine of these signed the completed document.

It was nine months before nine states had ratified, and the last of the key states was not included until a month later, when the New York convention ratified by a vote of thirty to twenty-seven. To the "miracle of Philadelphia" one must therefore add "the miracle of ratification."

Ratification probably could not have been secured without a commitment to add a written bill of rights. The first ten amendments, which included the Bill of Rights, were ratified a little over three years after the Constitution itself.

That the Constitution was ratified is largely attributable to the fact that the principal leaders in the states were willing to vote for a document that failed to embody every one of their preferences. For example, influential Thomas Jefferson, who was in Paris negotiating a treaty and therefore did not serve as a delegate, felt strongly that a bill of rights should have been included in the original Constitution. But Jefferson still supported the Constitution because he felt it was the best available. Benjamin Franklin stated that view in these words: "When you assemble a number of men to have the advantage over their joint wisdom, you inevitably assemble with those men, all their prejudices, their passions, their errors of opinion, their local interests, and their selfish views. From such an assembly can a perfect production be expected? It therefore astonishes me, Sir, to find this system approaching so near to perfection as it does. . . . The opinions I have had of its errors, I sacrifice to the public good."[4]

In other words, one should not expect perfection—one certainly should not expect all of his personal preferences—in a document that must represent a consensus. One should not sulk over a representative body's failure to attain perfection. Americans are well advised to support the best that can be obtained in the circumstances that prevail. That is sound advice not only for the drafting of a constitution but also for the adoption and administration of laws under it.

Inspiration

It was a miracle that the Constitution could be drafted and ratified. But what is there in the text of the Constitution that is divinely inspired?

Reverence for the United States Constitution is so great that sometimes individuals speak as if its every word and phrase had the same standing as scripture. Personally, I have never considered it necessary to defend every line of the Constitution as scriptural. For example, I find nothing scriptural in the compromise on slavery or the minimum age or years of citizenship for congressmen, senators, or the president. President J. Reuben Clark, who referred to the Constitution as "part of my religion,"[5] also said that it was not part of his belief or the doctrine of the Church that the Constitution was a "fully grown document." "On the contrary," he said, "we believe it must grow and develop to meet the changing needs of an advancing world."[6]

That was also the attitude of the Prophet Joseph Smith. He faulted the Constitution for not being "broad enough to cover the whole ground." In an obvious reference to the national government's lack of power to intervene when the state of Missouri used its militia to expel the Latter-day Saints from their lands, Joseph Smith said: "Its sentiments are good, but it provides no means of enforcing them. . . . Under its provision, a man or a people who are able to protect themselves can get along well enough; but those who have the misfortune to be weak or unpopular are left to the merciless rage of popular fury."[7] This omission of national power to protect citizens against state action to deprive them of constitutional rights was remedied in the Fourteenth Amendment, adopted just after the Civil War.

I see divine inspiration in what President J. Reuben Clark called the "great fundamentals" of the Constitution. In his many talks on the Constitution, he always praised three fundamentals: (a) the separation of powers into three independent branches of government in a federal system; (b) the essential freedoms of speech, press, and religion embodied in the Bill of Rights; and (c) the equality of all men before the law. I concur in these three, but I add two more. On my list there are five great fundamentals.

1. *Separation of powers.* The idea of separation of powers was at least a century old. The English Parliament achieved an initial separation of legislative and executive authority when they wrested certain powers from the king in the revolution of 1688. The concept of separation of powers became well established in the American colonies. State constitutions adopted during the Revolution distinguished between the executive, legislative, and judicial functions. Thus, a document commenting on the proposed Massachusetts Constitution of 1778 speaks familiarly of the principle "that the legislative, judicial, and executive powers are to be lodged in different hands, that each branch is to be independent, and further, to be so balanced, and be able to exert such checks upon the others, as will preserve it from dependence on, or a union with them."[8]

Thus we see that the inspiration on the *idea* of separation of powers came long before the U.S. Constitutional Convention. The inspiration in the convention was in its original and remarkably successful adaptation of the idea of separation of powers to the practical needs of a national government. The delegates found just the right combination to assure the integrity of each branch, appropriately checked and balanced with the others. As President Clark said: "It is this union of independence and dependence of these branches—legislative, executive and judicial—and of the governmental functions possessed by each of them, that constitutues the marvelous genius of this unrivalled document. . . . As I see it, it was here that the divine inspiration came. It was truly a miracle."[9]

2. *A written bill of rights.* This second great fundamental came by amendment, but I think Americans all look upon the Bill of Rights as part of the inspired work of the founding fathers. The

idea of a bill of rights was not new. Once again, the inspiration was in the brilliant, practical implementation of preexisting principles. Almost six hundred years earlier, King John had subscribed the Magna Charta, which contained a written guarantee of some rights for certain of his subjects. The English Parliament had guaranteed individual rights against royal power in the English Bill of Rights of 1689. Even more recently, some of the charters used in the establishment of the American colonies had written guarantees of liberties and privileges, with which the delegates were familiar.

I have always felt that the United States Constitution's closest approach to scriptural stature is in the phrasing of our Bill of Rights. Without the free exercise of religion, America could not have served as the host nation for the restoration of the gospel, which began just three decades after the Bill of Rights was ratified. I also see scriptural stature in the concept and wording of the freedoms of speech and press, the right to be secure against unreasonable searches and seizures, the requirements that there must be probable cause for an arrest and that accused persons must have a speedy and public trial by an impartial jury, and the guarantee that a person will not be deprived of life, liberty, or property without due process of law. President Ezra Taft Benson has said, "Reason, necessity, tradition, and religious conviction all lead me to accept the divine origin of these rights."[10]

The Declaration of Independence had posited these truths to be "self-evident," that all men "are endowed by their Creator with certain inalienable Rights," and that governments are instituted "to secure these Rights." This inspired Constitution was established to provide a practical guarantee of these God-given rights (see D&C 101:77), and the language implementing that godly objective is scriptural to me.

3. *Division of powers*. Another inspired fundamental of the U.S. Constitution is its federal system, which divides government powers between the nation and the various states. Unlike the inspired adaptations mentioned earlier, this division of sovereignty was unprecedented in theory or practice. In a day when

it is fashionable to assume that the government has the power and means to right every wrong, we should remember that the U.S. Constitution limits the national government to the exercise of powers expressly granted to it. The Tenth Amendment provides:

"The powers not delegated to the United States by the Constitution, nor prohibited to it by the States, are reserved to the States respectively or to the people."

This principle of limited national powers, with all residuary powers reserved to the people or to the state and local governments, which are most responsive to the people, is one of the great fundamentals of the U.S. Constitution.

The particular powers that are reserved to the states are part of the inspiration. For example, the power to make laws on personal relationships is reserved to the states. Thus, laws of marriage and family rights and duties are state laws. This would have been changed by the proposed Equal Rights Amendment (E.R.A.). When the First Presidency opposed the E.R.A., they cited the way it would have changed various legal rules having to do with the family, a result they characterized as "a moral rather than a legal issue."[11] I would add my belief that the most fundamental legal and political objection to the proposed E.R.A. was that it would effect a significant reallocation of law-making power from the states to the federal government.

4. *Popular sovereignty.* Perhaps the most important of the great fundamentals of the inspired Constitution is the principle of popular sovereignty: The people are the source of government power. Along with many religious people, Latter-day Saints affirm that God gave the power to the people, and the people consented to a constitution that delegated certain powers to the government. Sovereignty is not inherent in a state or nation just because it has the power that comes from force of arms. Sovereignty does not come from the divine right of a king, who grants his subjects such power as he pleases or is forced to concede, as in Magna Charta. The sovereign power is in the people. I believe this is one of the great meanings in the revelation which tells us that God established the Constitution of the United States,

> That every man may act . . . according to the moral agency which I have given unto him, that every man may be accountable for his own sins in the day of judgment.
>
> Therefore, it is not right that any man should be in bondage one to another.
>
> And for this purpose have I established the Constitution of this land. (D&C 101:78–80.)

In other words, the most desirable condition for the effective exercise of God-given moral agency is a condition of maximum freedom and responsibility. In this condition men are accountable for their own sins and cannot blame their political conditions on their bondage to a king or a tyrant. This condition is achieved when the people are sovereign, as they are under the Constitution God established in the United States. From this it follows that the most important words in the United States Constitution are the words in the preamble: "We, the people of the United States . . . do ordain and establish this Constitution."

President Ezra Taft Benson expressed the fundamental principle of popular sovereignty when he said, "We [the people] are superior to government and should remain master over it, not the other way around."[12] The Book of Mormon explains that principle in these words:

> An unrighteous king doth pervert the ways of all righteousness. . . .
>
> Therefore, choose you by the voice of this people, judges, that ye may be judged according to the laws. . . .
>
> Now it is not common that the voice of the people desireth anything contrary to that which is right; but it is common for the lesser part of the people to desire that which is not right; therefore this shall ye observe and make it your law—to do your business by the voice of the people. (Mosiah 29:23–26.)

Popular sovereignty necessarily implies popular *responsibility*. Instead of blaming their troubles on a king or other sovereign, all citizens must share the burdens and responsibilities of governing.

As the Book of Mormon teaches, "The burden should come upon all the people, that every man might bear his part." (Mosiah 29:34.)

President Clark's third great fundamental was the equality of all men before the law. I believe that to be a corollary of popular sovereignty. When power comes from the people, there is no legitimacy in legal castes or classes or in failing to provide all citizens the equal protection of the laws.

The delegates to the Constitutional Convention did not originate the idea of popular sovereignty, since they lived in a century when many philosophers had argued that political power originated in a social contract. But the United States Constitution provided the first implementation of this principle. After two centuries in which Americans may have taken popular sovereignty for granted, it is helpful to be reminded of the difficulties in that pioneering effort.

To begin with, a direct democracy was impractical for a country of four million people and about a half million square miles. As a result, the delegates had to design the structure of a constitutional, representative democracy, what they called "a Republican Form of Government."[13]

The delegates also had to resolve whether a constitution adopted by popular sovereignty could be amended, and if so, how.

Finally, the delegates had to decide how minority rights could be protected when the government was, by definition, controlled by the majority of the sovereign people.

A government based on popular sovereignty must be responsive to the people, but it must also be stable or it cannot govern. A constitution must therefore give government the power to withstand the cries of a majority of the people in the short run, though it must obviously be subject to their direction in the long run.

Without some government stability against an outraged majority, government could not protect minority rights. As President Clark declared: "The Constitution was framed in order to protect minorities. That is the purpose of written constitutions. In order that the minorities might be protected in the matter of amendments under our Constitution, the Lord required that the amendments should be made only through the operation of very large majorities—two-thirds for action in the Senate, and three-fourths as among the states. This is the inspired, prescribed order."[14]

The delegates to the Constitutional Convention achieved the required balance between popular sovereignty and stability through a power of amendment that was ultimately available but deliberately slow. Only in this way could the government have the certainty of stability, the protection of minority rights, and the potential of change, all at the same time.

To summarize, I see divine inspiration in these four great fundamentals of the U.S. Constitution:

- the separation of powers in the three branches of government;
- the Bill of Rights;
- the division of powers between the states and the federal government; and
- the application of popular sovereignty.

5. *The rule of law and not of men.* Further, there is divine inspiration in the fundamental underlying premise of this whole constitutional order. All the blessings enjoyed under the United States Constitution are dependent upon the rule of law. That is why President J. Reuben Clark said, "Our allegiance run[s] to the Constitution and to the principles which it embodies and not to individuals."[15] The rule of law is the basis of liberty.

As the Lord declared in modern revelation, constitutional laws are justifiable before him, "and the law also maketh you free." (D&C 98:5–8.) The self-control by which citizens subject themselves to law strengthens the freedom of all citizens and honors the divinely inspired Constitution.

CITIZEN RESPONSIBILITIES

U.S. citizens have an inspired Constitution, and therefore, what? Does the belief that the U.S. Constitution is divinely inspired affect citizens' behavior toward law and government? It should and it does.

U.S. citizens should follow the First Presidency's counsel to study the Constitution.[16] They should be familiar with its great fundamentals: the separation of powers, the individual guarantees in the Bill of Rights, the structure of federalism, the sovereignty of the people, and the principles of the rule of the law. They should oppose any infringement of these inspired fundamentals.

They should be law-abiding citizens, supportive of national, state, and local governments. The twelfth Article of Faith declares: "We believe in being subject to kings, presidents, rulers, and magistrates, in obeying, honoring, and sustaining the law."

The Church's official declaration of belief states:

> We believe that governments were instituted of God for the benefit of man; and that he holds men accountable for their acts in relation to them. . . .
> We believe that all men are bound to sustain and uphold the respective governments in which they reside. (D&C 134:1, 5.)

Those who enjoy the blessings of liberty under a divinely inspired constitution should promote morality, and they should practice what the founding fathers called "civic virtue." In his address on the U.S. Constitution, President Ezra Taft Benson quoted this important observation by John Adams, the second president of the United States: "Our Constitution was made only for a moral and religious people. It is wholly inadequate to the government of any other."[17]

Similarly, James Madison, who is known as the "Father of the Constitution," stated his assumption that there had to be "sufficient virtue among men for self-government." He argued in the *Federalist Papers* that "republican government presupposes the existence of these qualities in a higher degree than any other form."[18]

It is part of our civic duty to be moral in our conduct toward all people. There is no place in responsible citizenship for dishonesty or deceit or for willful law-breaking of any kind. We believe with the author of Proverbs that "righteousness exalteth a nation: but sin is a reproach to any people." (Proverbs 14:34.) The personal righteousness of citizens will strengthen a nation more than the force of its arms.

Citizens should also be practitioners of civic virtue in their conduct toward government. They should be ever willing to fulfill the duties of citizenship. This includes compulsory duties like military service and the numerous voluntary actions they must take if they are to preserve the principle of limited government through citizen self-reliance. For example, since U.S. citizens value the right of trial by jury, they must be willing to serve on juries, even those involving unsavory subject matter. Citizens who favor morality cannot leave the enforcement of moral laws to jurors who oppose them.

The single word that best describes a fulfillment of the duties of civic virtue is patriotism. Citizens should be patriotic. My favorite prescription for patriotism is that of Adlai Stevenson: "What do we mean by patriotism in the context of our times? . . . A patriotism that puts country ahead of self; a patriotism which is not short, frenzied outbursts of emotion, but the tranquil and steady dedication of a lifetime."[19]

I close with a poetic prayer. It is familiar to everyone in the United States, because the U.S. citizens sing it in one of their loveliest hymns. It expresses gratitude to God for liberty, and it voices a prayer that He will continue to bless them with the holy light of freedom:

> Our fathers' God, to thee,
> Author of liberty,
> To thee we sing;
> Long may our land be bright
> With freedom's holy light.
> Protect us by thy might,
> Great God, our King![20]

Notes

1. See "The Constitution," *Wilson Quarterly*, Spring 1987, pp. 97, 126.

2. Letter from Washington to Lafayette, 7 Feb. 1788, quoted in Catherine Drinker Bowen, *Miracle at Philadelphia*, Boston: Little, Brown, and Co., 1966, p. xvii.

3. Quoted in William O. Nelson, *The Charter of Liberty*, Salt Lake City: Deseret Book Co., 1987, p. 44.

4. *Notes of the Debates in the Federal Convention of 1787 Reported by James Madison*, p. 653, quoted in Nelson, *The Charter of Liberty*, p. 57.

5. J. Reuben Clark, Jr., *Stand Fast by Our Constitution*, Salt Lake City: Deseret Book Co., 1973, pp. 7, 172.

6. J. Reuben Clark, Jr., quoted in Martin B. Hickman, "J. Reuben Clark, Jr.: the Constitution and the Great Fundamentals," in Ray C. Hillam, ed., *"By the Hands of Wise Men,"* Provo, Utah: Brigham Young University Press, 1979, p. 53.

7. *History of the Church*, 6:57.

8. Quoted in Gerhard Casper, "Constitutionalism," *Occasional Papers from the Law School*, The University of Chicago, no. 22 (1987).

9. *Church News*, 29 November 1952, p. 12, quoted in Hillam, *"By the Hands of Wise Men,"* p. 48.

10. Ezra Taft Benson, *The Constitution, a Heavenly Banner*, Salt Lake City: Deseret Book Co., 1986, p. 6.

11. First Presidency letter of 12 October 1978.

12. Benson, *The Constitution, a Heavenly Banner*, p. 7.

13. U.S. Constitution, Art. IV, Sec. 4.

14. *J. Reuben Clark: Selected Papers on Religion, Education, and Youth*, ed. David H. Yarn, Jr., Provo, Utah: Brigham Young University Press, 1984, p. 165.

15. Ibid., p. 43.

16. First Presidency letter of 15 January 1987.

17. Benson, *The Constitution, a Heavenly Banner*, p. 23.

18. *The Federalist*, no. 55.

19. Adlai Stevenson, speech given in New York City, 27 August 1952, quoted in John Bartlett, *Familiar Quotations*, Boston: Little, Brown and Co., 1955, p. 986.

20. *Hymns* (1985), no. 339.

I NOW MAKE IT MY EARNEST prayer, that God would . . . incline the hearts of the citizens to cultivate a spirit of subordination and obedience to government, to entertain a brotherly affection and love for one another, . . . and finally, that he would most graciously be pleased to dispose us all, to do justice, to love mercy, and to demean ourselves with that charity, humility and pacific temper of mind, which were the characteristics of the Divine Author of our blessed religion, and without an humble imitation of whose example in these things, we can never hope to be a happy nation.

—GEORGE WASHINGTON

3

America Must Look to God
President Gordon B. Hinckley

It is a great privilege to be with you on this Sabbath evening when we gather in appreciation for the blessings we enjoy in this good land.

I commend most warmly those who work each year to stage Provo's great Freedom Festival. President Benson spoke at this podium two years ago in a moving eulogy on the Constitution and the founding fathers of our nation. Elder Dallin H. Oaks spoke a year ago on the remarkable provisions of our Constitution, which have provided liberty for the people and progress for the nation.

Tonight I hope you will join with me in an expression of appreciation to the Almighty for this choice and wonderful nation, which in effect is His creation; and also in a prayer for its strength and progress as it enters its third century.

A week ago today I returned home, having been in the British Isles and Israel, and having stopped briefly in Paris while en route from Jerusalem. As many of you know, the best part of any long journey is coming home, particularly when that journey is from another land.

Address given 26 June 1988.

As we flew across the Atlantic there came into my mind the words of Henry Van Dyke written many years ago:

'Tis fine to see the Old World, and travel up and down
Among the famous palaces and cities of renown,
To admire the crumbly castles and the statues of the kings,—
But now I think I've had enough of antiquated things.

So it's home again, and home again, America for me!
My heart is turning home again, and there I long to be
In the land of youth and freedom beyond the ocean bars,
Where the air is full of sunlight and the flag is full of stars.

I share with you a great love for this my native land. I have been around this world again and again. I have traveled across the seas south and west and east. I have wondered at the marvelous symmetry of Fujiyama in Japan. I have seen the Taj Mahal by moonlight in Agra, India. I have marveled at the transcendent beauty of the great mountains of Switzerland, France, and Italy. I have seen the orchards of Russia in the bloom of spring, the rice lands of China at harvest time. I have admired the pampas of Argentina and the towering peaks of Bolivia. I have walked the streets of the great and beautiful cities of Europe. I have done all of this and much more. And I have returned each time with a peculiar love for this my homeland.

I love America for her great and brawny strength, the products of her vital factories, and the science of her laboratories. I love her for the great intellectual capacity of her people. I love her for their generous hearts. I love her for her tremendous spiritual strengths. She is unique among the nations of the earth—in her discovery, in her birth as a nation, in the amalgamation of the races that have come to her shores, in the consistency and strength of her government, in the goodness of her people.

We first visited Jerusalem long ago, before the 1967 war. It was then a divided city. We retained the services of a guide who was an Arab. We stood on an elevation where we could see the other side of Jerusalem. With tears in his eyes he pointed to the home of which he had been dispossessed. And then he said with deep emotion: "You belong to the greatest nation on the face of the earth. Yours is the only nation which has been victorious in war and never claimed any territory as a prize of conquest.

"Your people have given millions, yes billions, to the poor of the earth and never asked for anything in return."

That I learned from a man in Jerusalem. I had never thought of it before. It is tremendously significant. I have stood in the American military cemetery in Suresnes, France, where are buried some who died in the First World War. It is a quiet and hallowed place, a remembrance of great sacrifice "to make the world safe for democracy." No additional territory was claimed by America as recompense for the sacrifices of those buried there.

I have stood in reverent awe and wonder in the beautiful American military cemetery on the outskirts of Manila in the Philippines. Here, standing row on row in perfect symmetry, are marble crosses and the Star of David marking the burial places of some 17,000 Americans who lost their lives in the Second World War. Surrounding that sacred ground are stone colonnades on which are incised the names of another 35,000 who were lost in the battles of the Pacific during that terrible conflict. There was victory, but not a claim for territory.

I have been up and down South Korea from the 38th parallel on the north to Pusan on the south and seen the ridges and the valleys where Americans fought and died, not to save their own land but to preserve freedom for people who were strangers to them but whom they acknowledged to be brothers under the fatherhood of God. Not an inch of territory was sought or added to the area of the United States during that conflict.

I have been up and down South Vietnam in the days of war, during those years when 55,000 Americans died in the sultry heat of that strange and foreign place fighting in the cause of human liberty without ambition for territory.

In no instance—in the First World War, in the Second World War, in the Korean War, in the Vietnam struggle—did this nation seek or seize territory for itself as a prize of conquest.

I love America for the tremendous genius of its scientists, its researchers, its laboratories, its universities, and the tens of thousands of facilities devoted to the increase of human health and comfort, to the sustenance of life, to improved communication and transportation. Its great throbbing industries have blessed the entire world. The standard of living of its people has been the envy of the entire earth. Its farmlands have yielded an abundance undreamed of in many other places. The entrepreneurial environment in which has grown its industry has been the envy of all nations.

I love America for its great spiritual strength. It is a land of churches and synagogues, of temples and tabernacles, of pulpits and altars. More than a century ago a young Frenchman, Alexis de Tocqueville, came here to observe this nation. After doing so he wrote:

> I sought for the greatness and genius of America in her commodious harbors and her ample rivers, and it was not there; in her fertile fields and boundless prairies, and it was not there; in her rich mines and her vast world commerce, and it was not there. Not until I went to the churches of America and heard her pulpits aflame with righteousness did I understand the secret of her genius and power. America is great because she is good, and if America ever ceases to be good, America will cease to be great.

This, I believe, is the core of the whole matter.

This is the great challenge now faced by this nation as we commence the third century under the Constitution that was written in the sultry summer of 1787 and ratified some nine months later on June 21, 1788, when New Hampshire passed her resolution of ratification.

Today we face challenges we have scarcely known in the past. We have come through wars, both civil and international, with victory and found peace. Now we are a people of contention, with strident and accusatory voices heard in argument across the nation. We rose from scratch to become the greatest industrial power in the history of the earth. Now we have lost much of our competitive edge and have seen other nations move ahead of us in various fields in both research and production. We spend millions upon millions of our resources in litigation one against another. Our spiritual power is sapped by a floodtide of pornography, by a debilitating epidemic of the use of narcotics and drugs that destroy both body and mind.

We are forgetting God, whose commandments we have put aside and obey not. In all too many ways we have substituted human sophistry for the wisdom of the Almighty.

I recently clipped a column from *U.S. News and World Report* written by Richard Lamm, former governor of Colorado. Said he:

"The reason the U.S. cannot compete in the new international economy is that our society itself has become uncompetitive. Better management and improved education are not enough to restore America's edge.

"Consider the handicaps we have built into our system:

"The U.S. spends almost 12 percent of the gross national product on health care—far more than any of our international competitors. U.S. auto makers, for example, spend as much as eight times more on employee health benefits than their Japanese counterparts. The irony is that we are far from being the healthiest people on earth.

"We are the most violent, crime-ridden society in the industrialized world. None of our competitors suffers as much crime-related loss or spends as much to guard against crime as American industry must.

"The U.S. is the world's most litigious society. Two thirds of the lawyers on this planet ply their trade here. No other society spends as much time in court or as much money defending and insuring itself against lawsuits.

"No modern, industrialized society has the rate of drug addiction, teenage pregnancy and functional illiteracy that we do. . . ."

He continues: "The American political system carries a 'for sale' sign. Winning office more often than not comes down to money, not ideas."

He concludes: "America is becoming uncompetitive because, in the words of the Roman historian Livy, 'We can bear neither our ills nor their cures.'" (*U.S. News and World Report,* April 25, 1988, p. 9).

Since the founding of the Republic the roots of our nation have drawn nurture from the waters of faith in God. "In God we trust" is the motto that appears on our money. As we face into the third century of our national life, it is time that we renewed our spiritual anchors. "Look to God and live," said an ancient prophet. As it was then, so it is today. "God Bless America" is the song we sing with reverence and pleading. Those blessings will come only as we deserve them. The inspired men who wrote our Constitution were raised up by the God of heaven "unto this very purpose." Can we expect peace and prosperity, harmony and goodwill while turning our backs on the source of our strength?

George Washington in his farewell address declared:

> Of all the dispositions and habits which lead to political prosperity, religion and morality are indispensible supports. In vain would that man claim the tribute of patriotism who should labor to subvert these great pillars of human happiness—these firmest props of the duties of men and citizens.
>
> The mere politician, equally with the pious man, ought to respect and to cherish them. . . .
>
> It is substantially true that virtue or morality is a necessary spring of popular government. This rule indeed extends with more or less force to every species of free government. (Quoted by J. Reuben Clark in *Stand Fast By Our Constitution* [Salt Lake City: Deseret Book, 1973], p. 27.)

Declared the Psalmist: "Blessed is the nation whose God is the Lord" (Psalm 33:12).

An acknowledgment of the Almighty and a return to the teachings of God will do more than all else to keep our ship of state on a steady course as she sails into the third century of nationhood. Here is the answer to the conflicts that beset us. Here is the answer to the evils of pornography, abortion, drugs, and the squandering of our resources on evil pursuits. Here is the answer to the great epidemic of litigation that consumes time, saps our financial strength, and shackles our entrepreneurial spirit. Here is the answer to tawdry politics that place selfish interest above the common good. As in de Tocqueville's day the strength and prosperity of the nation will not be found in her resources or her industries, unless also her pulpits are aflame with righteousness and her people bow in reverence before the Creator and Ruler of the universe.

Wisely, and with inspiration from on high, did the founding fathers safeguard those pulpits with the opening language of the Bill of Rights: "Congress shall make no law respecting an establishment of religion, or prohibiting the free exercise thereof" (Article 1 of the Bill of Rights).

That basic provision is now being challenged in the Congress and in the courts. There are threats real and dangerous. We here assembled, of all people, recognize and reverence the importance of freedom of worship.

Most of us, under an article of our faith, "claim the privilege of worshiping Almighty God according to the dictates of our own conscience, and allow all men the same privilege, let them worship how, where, or what they may" (11th Article of Faith).

Let the pulpits of all churches ring with righteousness. Let people everywhere bow in reverence before the Almighty, who is our one true strength. Let us look inward and adjust our priorities and standards. Let us look outward in the spirit of the Golden Rule. If we will do so in significant numbers across the land something marvelous will begin to happen.

I read with great interest a talk recently given by Margaret Thatcher, Prime Minister of Britain. She addressed the general assembly of the Church of Scotland. She spoke on self-reliance and personal responsibility as an expression of Christian principle. Among other things she said: "Any set of social and economic arrangements which is not founded on the acceptance of individual responsibility will do nothing but harm. We are all responsible for our own actions. We cannot blame society if we disobey the law. We simply cannot delegate the exercise of mercy and generosity to others."

She spoke of "the basic ties of the family, which are at the heart of our society and are the very nursery of civic virtue."

She went on to say: "The Christian religion—which, of course, embodies many of the great spiritual and moral truths of Judaism—is a fundamental part of our national heritage. For centuries it has been our very lifeblood. Indeed, we are a nation whose ideals are founded on the Bible. Also, it is quite impossible to understand our history or literature without grasping this fact. . . .

"The truths of the Judaic–Christian tradition are infinitely precious, not only, as I believe, because they are true, but also because they provide the moral impulse which alone can lead to that peace, in the true meaning of the word, for which we all long."

She continued: "There is little hope for democracy if the hearts of men and women in democratic societies cannot be touched by a call to something greater than themselves. Political structures, state institutions, collective ideals are not enough. We parliamentarians can legislate for the rule of law. You of the church can teach the life of faith." (Quoted in *Wall Street Journal*, May 31, 1988.)

Such the words of the British Prime Minister. They are as pertinent for us in this nation, whose ideals came of the great standards and teachings of the Bible, both the Old Testament and the New.

It was said anciently that "righteousness exalteth a nation: but sin is a reproach to any people" (Proverbs 14:34).

We who believe in the Book of Mormon are conscious of great blessings prophesied for the land of America. "Behold, this is a choice land, and whatsoever nation shall possess it shall be free from bondage, and from captivity, and from all other nations under heaven, if they will but serve the God of the land, who is Jesus Christ" (Ether 2:12).

May all of us here assembled resolve to lift our voice for truth and goodness in the land, and offer our supplications to our Eternal Father. May we gratefully acknowledge our Father's inspiration in the Declaration of Independence of 1776 and in the Constitution of 1787. And may we ourselves be worthy children of God as we pray for the people of this land, that hearts may be touched, that peace may prevail, and that righteousness may spread across our nation.

LIBERTY EXISTS IN PROPORTION to wholesome restraint.
—DANIEL WEBSTER

4

The Country with a Conscience
ELDER BOYD K. PACKER

When we lived in New England, there were two historic sites we visited as often as we could. Each inspired a deep feeling of reverence. The first, the birthplace of the Prophet Joseph Smith at South Royalton, Vermont; the other, the Old North Bridge at Concord, Massachusetts, where the never-ending struggle for independence began.

At Concord you follow the Battle Lane through the trees toward the bridge. A few yards in on the left is a small marker missed by most who go there. It marks the grave of two British soldiers. The small plaque reads:

> They came three thousand miles and died
> To keep the past upon the throne;
>
> Unheard, beyond the ocean tide,
> Their English mother made her moan.
>
> —James Russell Lowell

Address given 25 June 1989.

From this distance it does not offend one's patriotism to feel some deep compassion for those who then were the enemy. Time rearranges our prejudices and enemies become allies.

But it takes time for feelings to mellow. One early American historian describing the Battle of Bunker Hill said, "Three times in the face of the withering fire, the cowardly British charged up the hill."

Closer to the bridge is the Memorial Shaft. The monument was dedicated in 1837. Ralph Waldo Emerson, who lived in the neighborhood, wrote his famous Concord Hymn for the occasion. Across the bridge, where the farmers made their stand, is the statue cast from old cannons of the minuteman, a colonial farmer depicted leaving his plow, musket in hand. It was dedicated in 1875. President Ulysses S. Grant, his cabinet, and the governors from all New England were present. Emerson's words are engraved on the base of the statue. Let me recite them for you. They are well worth memorizing.

The Concord Hymn

By the rude bridge that arched the flood,
Their flag to April's breeze unfurled,
Here once the embattled farmers stood
And fired the shot heard round the world.

The foe long since in silence slept;
Alike the conqueror silent sleeps;
And Time the ruined bridge has swept
Down the dark stream that seaward creeps.

On this green bank, by this soft stream,
We set today a votive stone;
That memory may their deed redeem,
When, like our sires, our sons are gone.

Spirit, that made these heroes dare
To die, and leave their children free,

> Bid Time and Nature gentle spare
> The shaft we raise to them and thee.
>
> —Ralph Waldo Emerson

George Washington was not at Concord Bridge, nor was anyone else you can name. They were the anonymous rank and file of colonists who wore no uniforms, were untrained for combat, and carried nondescript weapons never intended for military action.

At the dedication of the Minuteman statue, George William Curtis said of them:

> The minuteman of the Revolution!—he was the old, the middle-aged, and the young. He was Captain Miles of Concord, who said that he went to battle as he went to church. He was Captain Davis of Acton, who reproved his men for jesting on the march. He was Deacon Josiah Haynes of Sudbury, eighty years old, who marched with his company to the South Bridge at Concord, then joined in the hot pursuit to Lexington, and fell as gloriously as Warren at Bunker Hill. [We don't remember Warren, either.] He was James Hayward of Acton, twenty-two years old, foremost in that deadly race from Concord to Charlestown, who raised his piece at the same moment with a British soldier, each exclaiming, "You are a dead man!" The Briton dropped, shot through the heart. James Hayward fell mortally wounded. "Father," he said, "I started with forty balls; I have three left. I never did such a day's work before. Tell mother not to mourn too much; and tell her whom I love more than my mother, that I am not sorry I turned out."
>
> This was the minuteman of the Revolution, the rural citizen trained in the common school, the church, and the town-meeting; who carried a bayonet that thought, and whose gun, loaded with a principle, brought down, not a man, but a system. (Charles Eliot Norton, ed., *Orations and Addresses of George William Curtis* [New York: Harper & Brothers, 1894].)

However anonymous each may be, the great moments in history rest always on the rank and file of humankind. It was true then and it is true now.

Let me tell you of two whose names you have never before heard.

Peter Francisco

No one knows for sure where Peter Francisco came from. It is thought that he may have been kidnapped from the island of Terceira, in the Azores, by Portuguese sailors who hoped to sell him in the American colonies as an indentured servant. If that was the plan, something went wrong with it, because they abandoned him on the wharf at Hopewell, Virginia, a few miles downriver from Richmond. He was five years old.

He was taken into the home of Judge Anthony Winston, an uncle of Patrick Henry. Peter was present when the famous "Give me liberty or give me death" speech was given. It did something to the boy. He was sixteen years old and a strapping 6'6" when he joined Company 9 of the Virginia 10th Regiment on October 10, 1776.

His first fight was the ill-fated Battle of Brandywine Creek. He was wounded in the leg and removed to a Moravian farm house for treatment. General LaFayette was there being treated for a bullet wound. The general asked the boy if he could do something for him. Peter requested a sword big enough to match his physical stature. The general sent him one. It was five feet long.

Peter fought at Germantown and suffered through Valley Forge. At Monmouth he took a musket ball in his thigh. At the British stronghold at Stony Point he was the second man over the wall and fought on despite a nine-inch bayonet slash across his abdomen.

At nineteen he returned home with a musket ball in one of his legs. It would cause him pain the rest of his life. Within a year he had reenlisted and was fighting with the Virginia militia in the South. At Camden, South Carolina, the militia was defeated. Peter rescued a cannon and a colonel from behind enemy lines.

At Guilford Courthouse a British soldier stabbed through the calf of Peter's leg with a bayonet. Later another pierced his other leg at the knee, slicing all the way to the hipbone before Peter fell from his horse. He stayed conscious long enough to crawl to a tree. He was then twenty-one.

Near the end of the war he emerged from a tavern at Burkeville, Virginia, to face nine British soldiers who were scavenging for supplies. Peter was completely unarmed. While some of them looted the tavern, two soldiers held him at sword point. One of them took an interest in Peter's silver knee-buckles. Presently the soldier was dead and Peter held the sword. Six British survivors fled to the advanced guard of Tartleton's Legion. The entire guard, four hundred strong, retreated, not knowing that the "ambush" was only one man.

There is more, much more, but that should suffice. Question! Why isn't Peter Francisco remembered? Because he wasn't a general, even an officer. He was offered a battlefield commission but had to refuse—literacy was required for a commission. Peter Francisco could neither read nor write.

Peter lived to raise a family and died January 16, 1830. He was about seventy years old.

Mrs. Hendee

On October 16, 1780, about the time that Peter was routing the British at Burkeville Tavern, Robert Havens was awakened by the barking of a neighbor's dog; something was after the sheep. Partially clothed, he left his house near the White River in South Royalton, Vermont, and ascended the hill. He found the sheep safe. He stood pensively looking back as the first light of dawn touched his frontier home. Something was wrong!

As he turned to retrace his steps, he saw a large company of Indians move from the forest and push in the front door of his home. Two teenage boys who had been aroused to help with the sheep were getting dressed. One was his son Daniel Havens. The other, Thomas Pimber, was courting a neighbor girl and had stayed overnight with the Havens family.

The boys burst through the back door and ran for their lives. Daniel stumbled as he reached the stream, rolled down the bank under a log, and was not discovered. Thomas Pimber was not so fortunate. In a few minutes the Indians were roaring with delight. His scalp had a double cow-lick. Cut in two, it would fetch a double bounty from the British.

The Indians, three hundred from Canada, and a few Tories were commanded by a British captain named Horton. The British had offered them $8.00 each for live captive men, something less for boys, and a lesser amount for scalps. The British had placed no bounty on women and girls; they were therefore immune to captivity and subject to something less than death.

During that long-forgotten burning of South Royalton, Vermont, the Indians moved downriver capturing the men and boys, killing those who resisted. They killed all the livestock and burned the houses and barns holding the harvest upon which the colonists depended for survival during the long New England winter.

Some distance downstream, the Hendee family had been warned. The husband set out on foot to warn others downstream. Hannah Hendee grabbed her son Michael, who was seven, and a younger daughter and ran for the woods. Just when she thought she had reached safety, a band of Indians stepped from the shadows and wrested her boy from her. One of them spoke English. She demanded to know what they were going to do to her boy. The Indian replied, "Make a soldier of him."

As the Indians dragged her sobbing boy away, she made her way toward the road along the river carrying her little girl, who screamed in panic for her mother to keep the Indians away.

Near the river she met Captain Horton and asked what they intended to do with the little boys. She was told that they would be marched to Canada with the men. She said the youngsters could not endure such a march, and was told, "In that case, they will be killed."

She headed down the road toward Lebanon, sixteen miles away, carrying her little girl. She had not gone far when she was filled with a surge of uncommon resolve, a fierce determination. They could not keep her little boy!

She returned upriver and found the British and the Indians gathering their captives on the opposite bank. She started across and would have drowned had not an old Indian helped her to shore.

Oblivious of the danger, she demanded her little boy. Captain Horton said he could not control the Indians; it was none of his concern what they did. She threatened him: "You are their commander, and they *must* and will obey you. The curse will fall upon *you* for whatever crime *they* may commit, and all the innocent blood they shall here shed will be found in your skirts when the secrets of men's hearts are made known, and it will cry for vengeance upon your head!"

When her little son was brought in, she took him by the hand and refused to let go. An Indian threatened her with a cutlass and jerked her son away. She defiantly took him back and said that she would follow them every step of the way to Canada, she would never give up, they would not have her little boy!

Finally, intimidated by her determination, Captain Horton told her to take her son and leave. He could face an army of men but not a mother driven by the strongest of emotions. She had gone but a few rods when she was made to return. Captain Horton said she must wait in camp until all the captives were assembled and the march north began.

During the day other little boys were brought into camp. Desperately they clung to Mrs. Hendee. With uncommon courage she interceded for them as vigorously as she had for her own.

Finally, when the captives were assembled for the long march to Canada, Mrs. Hendee somehow crossed the river with her daughter and nine small boys: her son Michael; Roswell Parkhurst; Andrew and Sheldon Durkey; Joseph Ricks; Rufus Fish and his brother; Nathaniel Evans; and Daniel Downer.

Two of them she carried across. The others waded through the water with their arms around each other's necks, clinging to her skirts. As the cold October night closed in, Mrs. Hendee huddled in the woods with the soaking wet little brood she had rescued from certain death.

One of the boys, Daniel Downer, "received such an affright from the horrid crew, that he was ever afterwards unable to take care of himself, wholly unfit for business and lived for many years, wandering from place to place, a solemn, tho' silent witness of the distress and horror of that dreadful scene." (Evelyn Wood Lovejoy, *History of Royalton, Vermont* [Burlington, Vermont: Free Press Printing Co., 1911].)

> They talk about a woman's sphere,
> As though it has a limit;
>
> There's not a place in earth or heaven,
> There's not a task to mankind given,
>
> There's not a blessing nor a woe,
> There's not a whispered yes or no,
>
> There's not a life, or death, or birth,
> That has a feather's weight of worth . . .
>
> Without a woman in it.
> (Anon.)

Surely neither the famous Patrick Henry, who demanded liberty or death, nor the revered Nathan Hale, who regretted that he had but one life to give for his country, offered more than did Hannah Hendee, the long-forgotten mother from South Royalton, Vermont.

Mrs. Hendee was at war, inspired by the best of all causes, armed with nothing more than a clear conscience, justified by the highest principles of morality. War is a terrible, terrible thing, but there are times when the God of Heaven justifies a people in taking up arms. The Book of Mormon tells of Nephites locked in battle against a stronger enemy army who "did fight like dragons."

> Nevertheless [the record says], the Nephites were inspired by a better cause, for they were not fighting for monarchy nor power but they were fighting for their homes and their liberties, their wives and their children, and their all, yea, for their rites of worship and their church.
>
> And they were doing that which they felt was the duty which they owed to their God; for the Lord had said unto them, and also unto their fathers, that: Inasmuch as ye are not guilty of the first offense, neither the second, ye shall not suffer yourselves to be slain by the hands of your enemies.
>
> And again, the Lord has said that: Ye shall defend your families even unto bloodshed. Therefore for this cause were the Nephites contending with the Lamanites, to defend themselves, and their families, and their lands, their country, and their rights, and their religion. (Alma 43:45–47.)

Since that fateful day at Concord Bridge, few generations have passed in this land without a call to arms. Threats to our independence have reoccurred with persistent regularity.

It was only twenty-one years between the armistice in 1918 and September 1939, when World War II began! Who was it said, "The one thing we learn from history is that we don't learn anything from history"?

With little hestitation this nation has responded to threats to freedom with military action. Not only have we fought to protect our own independence but to secure or protect it for other nations as well.

Sustained by a courage that comes only from a moral people, we have fought for our homes and our families, our lands, our country, our rights, and our religion. "Chains," President David O. McKay said, "are worse than bayonets." (Conference Report, April 1955, p. 24.)

While we were never to a man "Simon Pure" and there have always been some of us bad enough not to deserve the title of a good, moral Christian people, there have always been enough of us who have been good enough to deserve it.

Strength that comes from decency, from morality, is the one, the essential ingredient required for the preservation of freedom, indeed for the preservation of humankind. And there is reason to believe that we are losing it.

Something changed. Perhaps for the first time since Concord Bridge, that balance of decency and morality is shifting past the center. The balance, which measures the morality of all of us put together, is slowly tipping in the wrong fatal direction. These lines written to describe another time and place seem to fit our circumstance now.

> That which they would never yield to military might,
> They threw away unwittingly
> When evil came by night
> And scattered tares among the grain.
> Nor did they rouse to see
> Their fundamental moral strength
> In mortal jeopardy.
> ("Ancestral Home" by Boyd K. Packer, from Donna S. Packer, *On Footings from the Past* [Salt Lake City: Bookcraft, 1988], p. 401.)

The war in Vietnam did something to us. We had the military might, the arms, the ammunition, the manpower, the planes and ships and instruments of war undreamed of in the past. But we could not conquer!

What happened did not happen at Danang or Saigon. It only

surfaced there. It happened first in and to the universities of America. It happened when agnostics and atheists were protected in teaching their philosophy of religion in public institutions of higher learning.

Because they claim affiliation with no church, the principle of separation of church and state is supposed not to apply to them. They are free to teach their faithless philosophy at public expense, to shake, even destroy, the faith of their students. Meanwhile teachers of faith are restrained and churches are kept off campus.

What happened, happened in and to the schools and the churches, to the towns and cities; it happened in the homes and in the hearts of the American people.

Some terrible things occurred in Vietnam. Our men had no stomach for it when they were doing it and could not get over it after it was done. Many fought without the conviction that what they were doing had a fundamental moral purpose.

It was different from the atomic bombs on Nagasaki and Hiroshima. Because of the slaughter occurring each day and the certainty of a horrible increase in casualties on *both* sides in an invasion of Japan, it had been argued, not without substance, that the loss of life on both sides would be less should the war be brought to an end. Even then, something was lost to humanity when that occurred, because the rank and file of humanity suffered.

It had been different in Korea as well, for we had our motives more securely in place. And what was to happen later to the moral fabric of our nation had not happened then.

Something has happened to our collective conscience. Countries have a conscience, you know, just like men do. Something in our national conscience became unsettled. A clouded conscience cannot conquer, not in the end it cannot. A clear conscience cannot be defeated, not in the end it cannot.

Something is weakening the moral fiber of the American people. We have always had couples live together without marriage, but we have not honored it as an acceptable lifestyle. We have always had children born out of wedlock, but we have never made it to be respectable. And we have never before regarded babies, conceived in wedlock or out, to be an inconvenience and destroyed them by the thousands through abortion. And this while barren couples yearn for a child to raise.

We have always had some who followed a life of perversion, but we have never before pushed through legislation to protect that way of life lest we offend the rights of an individual. We have never been this liberated before.

We have always had those who were guilty of criminal acts, but we have not put the rights of the accused above the rights of the victim.

If one single soul does not wish to listen for a moment to a public prayer, one which does not offend, even pleases the majority, we are told we must now eliminate prayer completely from all of public life.

We have always had addictive drugs, but not in the varieties we have now and not widely sold near public schools, even elementary schools. When perversion and addiction are justified as the expression of individual rights and call up a pestilence which threatens even the innocent, must the right of privacy preclude even testing to find where it is moving? What kind of individual freedom is this, anyway?

Did our young men die for this? We have always held the rights of the individual to be sovereign. But we have never before placed the collective rights of the majority in subjugation to the individual rights of any single citizen.

Any virtue, pressed to an extreme, becomes a vice; thrift becomes stinginess, generosity becomes wastefulness, self-confidence becomes pride, humility becomes weakness—and on and on. Individual rights as an ideal cannot endure except there be respect for the agency of others. There is no true freedom without responsibility. Freedom without restraint becomes tyranny of a new and fatal kind.

Freedom certainly cannot exist under a system where the citizens are stripped of individuality and pressed into the classless society by a despotic state, where men and women are compelled to exist as faceless worker bees. That is slavery!

Neither can freedom long survive in a society where the rights of the individual are fanatically promoted regardless of what happens to society itself. The rights of the individual, the ideal, the virtue, when pressed to the extreme, like other virtues, will presently become a vice. Without some balance, activists, lawyers, legislators, judges, and courts who think they are protecting individual freedom are in fact fabricating a new and subtle and sinister kind of dictatorship.

We have a present example:

A symbol is an object which represents something, which, though equally real, is not tangible. The flag is a symbol.

> When Freedom, from her mountain height,
>   Unfurled her standard to the air,
> She tore the azure robe of night,
>   And set the stars of glory there;
> She mingled with its gorgeous dyes
> The milky baldric of the skies,
> And striped its pure, celestial white
> With streakings of the morning light;
> Then, from his mansion in the sun,
> She called her eagle-bearer down,
> And gave into his mighty hand
> The symbol of her chosen land.
> (Joseph Rodman Drake, in *The World's Best Loved Poems*, James G. Lawson, ed., pp. 287–288.)

To destroy that symbol is to reject what it represents.

The burning of the flag is an act which in itself becomes symbolic. It symbolizes the rejection of the Pledge of Allegiance. The Bill of Rights guarantees freedom of speech. Speech is made up of spoken or printed words. Words are words are words. Acts are acts are acts.

The willful destruction of the flag which belongs to all of us is the act of an extremist. A court decision legalizing the destruction of it to protect the rights of one protestor is equally extreme.

The rights of the individual, though God-given, cannot be absolute simply because there are many individuals. Did not God himself counsel us to be temperate in all things? (Alma 7:23, 38:10, D&C 12:8.)

Freedom cannot survive in the face of this strange new despotism. But it can survive in a sensible society where extremes are pulled back into balance. We call that democracy. It is worth preserving. It is now in an ominous kind of danger.

The Book of Mormon says something about that.

> Choose you by the voice of this people, judges, that ye may be judged according to the laws which have been given you by our fathers, which are correct, and which were given them by the hand of the Lord.
>
> Now it is not common that the voice of the people desireth anything contrary to that which is right; but it is common for the lesser part of the people to desire that which is not right; therefore this shall ye observe and make it your law—to do your business by the voice of the people.
>
> And if the time comes that the voice of the people doth choose iniquity, then is the time that the judgments of God will come upon you; yea, then is the time he will visit you with great destruction even as he has hitherto visited this land. (Mosiah 29:25–27.)

It warns us as well to be alert during times of peace and prosperity:

> Yea, and we may see at the very time when he doth prosper his people, yea, in the increase of their fields, their flocks and their herds, and in gold, and in silver, and in all manner of precious things of every kind and art; sparing their lives, and delivering them out of the hands of their enemies; softening the hearts of their enemies that they should not declare wars against them; yea, and in fine, doing all things for the welfare and happiness of his people; yea, then is the time that they do harden

their hearts, and do forget the lord their God, and do trample under their feet the Holy One—yea, and this because of their ease, and their exceedingly great prosperity.

And thus we see that except the Lord doth chasten his people with many afflictions, yea, except he doth visit them with death and with terror, and with famine and with all manner of pestilence, they will not remember him. (Helaman 12:2–3.)

There must be enough of us who have faith enough and who are moral enough to desire that which is right. Virtues, like love and liberty and patriotism, do not exist in general, they exist in particular. If morality exists at all, it exists in the individual heart and mind of the ordinary citizen. Such virtues cannot be isolated in any other place; not in the rocks or in the water, not in trees or air, not in animals or birds. If it exists at all, it exists in the human heart. Morality flourishes when the rank and file are free. It flourishes where a conscience is clear, where men have faith in God and are obedient to the restraints He has set upon human conduct.

There is a light, a "true light, which lighteth every man that cometh into the world" (John 1:9). This light of Christ is the ingredient which binds the whole human family together and forms something of a universal conscience.

There is nothing that is right that we cannot achieve if our individual and our national conscience is clear.

Now what are we to do? Let me tell you:

Just go home and be decent, Sunday go-to-meeting people. Teach your children decency and honor, cooperation and tolerance, citizenship and patriotism. Teach them to be good. Teach them to have a clear conscience. Then we will produce a generation who will know what to do and have the courage to do it.

Eighty-year-old Deacon Josiah Haynes who fell at Concord, and twenty-two-year-old James Hayward whose last words to the girl he loved more than his mother were, "I'm not sorry I turned out," both had conviction and the courage to die for it. Peter Francisco in Virginia, Hannah Hendee in Vermont—both lived for it.

You live for it! Just be decent. Take care of your family, you yourself. Don't abandon that responsibility to the government, and don't let them take it from you. Go where virtue and morality and clear consciences are fostered. Go to church, do your part, pay your tithes and offerings, say your prayers, read the scriptures. Be a citizen, vote; in fact, pray and then vote. Then, when the crisis comes, and come it will, you and all the rest of us will know what is right and be willing to do what is right.

I see something else happening, something good. I see a resurgence of faith and decency. I see a restless public saying, "Hey now, we're getting close to the limit of some things." I see the rank and file joining to express a collective will. I hear them saying, "We've had enough of extremes. We want balanced, common, garden-variety democracy."

It has been prophesied that the Constitution of the United States will hang by a thread and that the elders of Israel will step forth to save it. (Journal History, July 4, 1854, Brigham Young; *Church News*, 15 December 1948.)

In my mind that does not require a few heroes in public office steering some saving legislation through the halls of Congress, neither some brilliant military leaders rallying our defense against an invading army. In my mind, that could well be the rank and file of men and women of faith who revere the Constitution and believe that the strength of democracy rests in the ordinary family and in each member of it. It rests with ordinary fathers and mothers who do not neglect the spiritual development of their children.

It rests with fathers and mothers who will send their sons and daughters to the four corners of the earth to teach that, "If [we will follow in his] word, then [we will be his] disciples indeed; and [we] shall know the truth and the truth shall make [us] free" (John 8:32).

Patrick and Nathan, we need you! George and Abraham, we need you! We need your heroic kind of patriotism! Josiah and Thomas and Peter and Hannah, we need you most of all. We need you right where you are, in ordinary towns living in ordinary homes, going to ordinary jobs, sending your children to ordinary schools, and taking them to ordinary churches to worship God. That will secure our moral fiber from which will come the extraordinary patriotism and the extraordinary faith to keep us free!

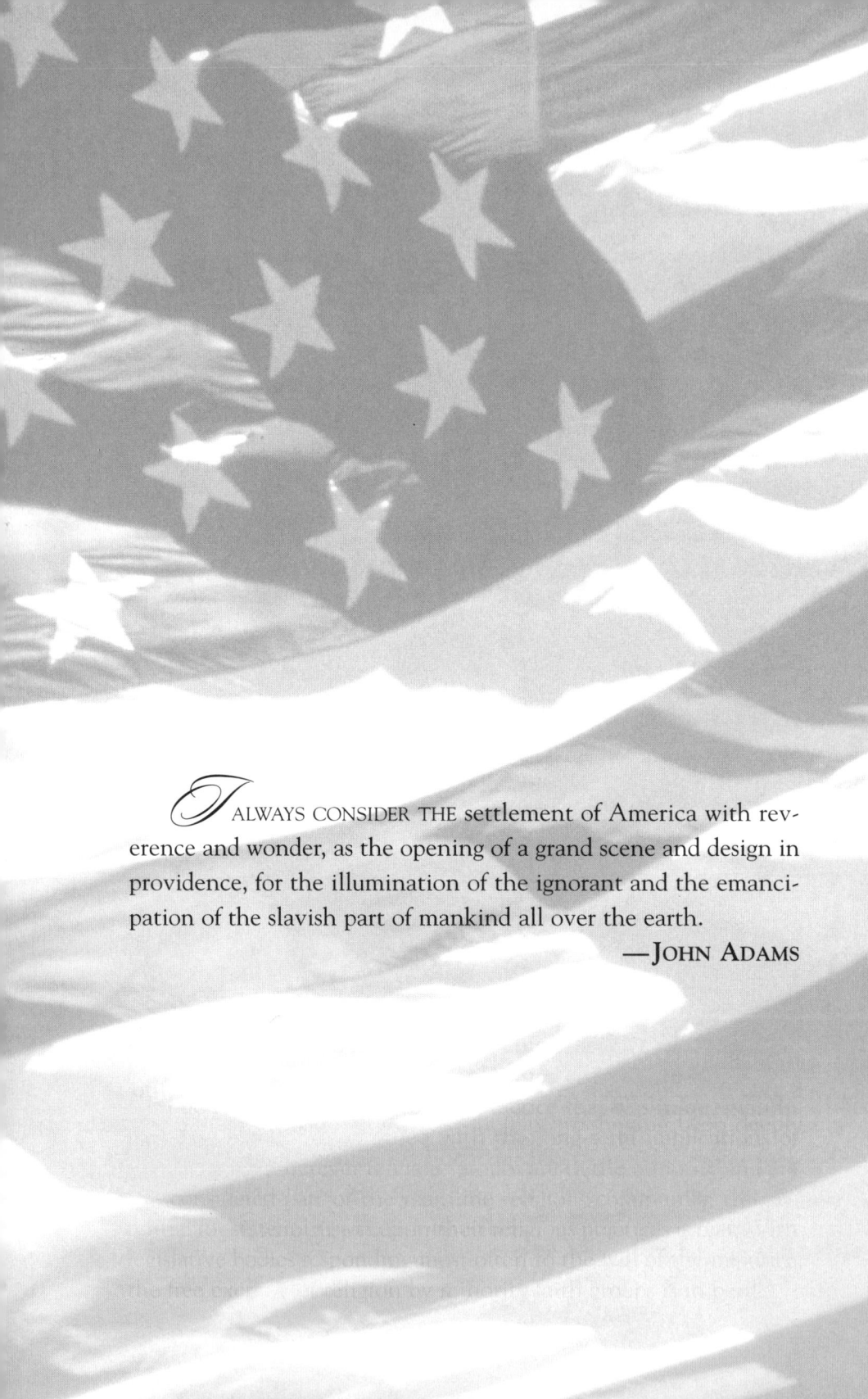

I always consider the settlement of America with reverence and wonder, as the opening of a grand scene and design in providence, for the illumination of the ignorant and the emancipation of the slavish part of mankind all over the earth.

—JOHN ADAMS

5

Liberty, License, and Law
ELDER RUSSELL M. NELSON

My dear companion, Dantzel, and I are deeply grateful for the privilege of being with you on this significant occasion. Perhaps as never before we sincerely rejoice in commemorating our heritage of freedom at this time of the year.

Many of us take our foundation of freedom for granted until it isn't there. Dantzel and I visited Havana, Cuba, thirty-eight years ago when, as tourists, we were enjoying the services of our English-speaking guide, whom we called George. He was driving us to see the sights of Havana when he was summoned to a stop by a policeman. When their animated Spanish conversation cooled off, George opened his wallet and paid some money to the police officer, who then went on his way. After we resumed our sightseeing, we asked George why he had been arrested. We were not aware of speeding or violation of any traffic law. We shall never forget George's reply.

He said something like this: "You folks from the U.S.A. are all alike. You don't understand your liberty. You live in a land governed by law. *That* gives you your freedom. Here in Havana our society is regulated by men. If I want to survive as a tourist

---

Address given 1 July 1990.

guide, I have to submit to requests of the police, even when I have done nothing wrong. The police officer merely notified me that if I wanted to continue to be your guide, I would have to pay him for that privilege."

We came away from that experience with a deeper appreciation for the Constitution of the United States of America, and for a government that provides liberty based on law.

Freedom festivals in our beloved country may be a little different this year. Since the last Fourth of July, remarkable political changes have taken place. In many nations of the earth, communism has fallen. Throughout the world, shouts of freedom fill the air. The old shell of spiritual confinement is being burst by newfound feelings of freedom. This gives additional cause for celebration tonight.

It is highly significant that the English language has these two wonderful words—*freedom* and *liberty*—to describe precious privileges that we enjoy. In contrast, most European languages have only one word, such as German, freiheit; French, liberte; or Russian, svoboda.

But we who love the word of God need not depend on the dictionary alone for our understanding of the concept of freedom. We can study the scriptures to gain spiritual insight. In analyzing the standard works in the English language, I find that the word *freedom* appears in thirty-three verses of holy scripture. Twenty-seven of those thirty-three verses are in the Book of Mormon. To me, it is quite remarkable that the number of verses with the terms *freedom* or *liberty* in the Book of Mormon is nearly double that of the other books of scripture combined!

May we cite a sample or two from the Book of Mormon:

Moroni was . . . a man whose soul did joy in the liberty and the freedom of his country (Alma 48:11).

Here is another:

Remember, remember, my brethren, that whosoever perisheth, perisheth unto himself; and whosoever doeth iniquity doeth it unto himself; for behold, ye are free; ye are permitted to act for yourselves; for behold, God hath given unto you a knowledge and he hath made you free (Helaman 14:30).

Biblical scriptures pertaining to liberty and freedom, though less numerous than those in the Book of Mormon, are just as precious. I especially treasure this passage from the book of Galatians:

Stand fast therefore in the liberty wherewith Christ hath made us free, and be not entangled again with the yoke of bondage (Galatians 5:1).

The Book of Mormon contains promises unique to this land of America:

This land is consecrated unto him whom [the Lord] shall bring. And if it so be that they shall serve him according to the commandments which he hath given, it shall be a land of liberty unto them. (2 Nephi 1:7; see also 2 Nephi 10:11–14; D&C 10:50–51.)

A similar promise was made to an earlier generation of Americans:

Behold, this is a choice land, and whatsoever nation shall possess it shall be free from bondage, and from captivity, and from all other nations under heaven, if they will but serve the God of the land, who is Jesus Christ (Ether 2:12).

Even with these marvelous scriptural insights, the fulness of freedom's glory is somewhat difficult to comprehend, especially by one who has never been without it.

Distinguished leaders have attempted to describe the limitations of democracy's relationship to freedom. Czechoslovakia's new president, Vaclav Havel, recently said: "As long as people are people, democracy in the full sense of the word will always be no more than an ideal" (Address to a joint session of the United States Congress, February 21, 1990).

Even Winston Churchill declared democracy as "the worst form of government, except all those other forms that have been tried from time to time" (House of Commons, 11 November 1947, cited in *The Oxford Dictionary of Quotations*, third edition, Oxford University Press, 1979, p. 150).

Freedom is, strictly speaking, not an absolute but a comparative idea. In a way, it is like health. Both freedom and health can be described with deep emotional conviction only by those who have known the contrast, having once been denied their freedom or their health.

A person who lies helplessly in a hospital bed hungers for health. Similarly, a person who cannot move because he is pinned under the weight of political confinement yearns for freedom much more than someone who has never known that awful feeling of constraint.

Democracy alone cannot promise perfect freedom, but its freedoms promise opportunity. And those freedoms legitimize the privilege of an individual's pursuit of happiness.

Yet freedom does nothing to guide that search. It is much easier to advocate freedom than it is to determine what to do with it. That is one of the challenges facing newly liberated countries.

Indeed, Fourth of July celebrations will be different this year. Throughout our lifetimes, many have understood freedom solely in terms of an ideological struggle. We have been taught to contrast freedom to bondage, liberty to totalitarianism, capitalism to communism, or democracy to despotism.

Now as communism has collapsed in some nations, and as new democracies have arisen, the tempo in the battle of ideology winds down. President Havel described 1989's "revolutionary changes in Europe as those which will enable us to escape from the rather antiquated straitjacket of this bi-polar view of the world" (Address to joint session of the United States Congress, February 21, 1990).

The remarkable crumbling of communism now brings us to a new era of freedom without the foe to which we have been accustomed virtually all of our lives. But as the zealous fervor for communism wanes, so might the zealous fervor for democracy also fade. That risk is real.

There is also another risk. It relates to personal freedom, which differs from the political freedom provided by democracy. And the risk stems from personal freedom's license too often misused. Here as well as abroad are evidences that precious personal freedoms are being surrendered. The warning signs are clear.

Personal freedom is lessened when pornography enters our homes. Personal freedom is eroded when legal and illegal drugs inflict harm on our loved ones. Addiction to such mental and physical snares causes one to surrender the freedom to choose. Pornography's parasitic power and the insidious incursion of drugs first endanger and then limit personal freedom. In time, they can literally disconnect an individual from his or her own will! Truly but sadly, personal freedom thus misused can be self-destructive.

I'll not say more about pornography, but I would like to comment further on our special moment in history when "freedom" to addict oneself through so-called "substance abuse" has spawned a new challenge to our society. Indeed, drugs have become the modern "mess of pottage" for which souls are sold. Friends and relatives near and dear are all at risk.

In December 1989 the American Medical Association declared that substance abuse was this country's number one public health problem. According to research data compiled by experts, legal drugs—such as alcohol and nicotine—and illegal drugs—such as cocaine and heroin—now contribute to approximately 25 percent of all deaths in the United States each year (David E. Smith, "Addiction Medicine," *The Western Journal of Medicine*, vol. 152, May 1990, p. 500).

What a travesty! In this land of the free and home of the brave, one death in four now comes from drugs!

It is odd that more people die of addiction to legal drugs than from the use of illicit drugs. In the United States of America, more than 350,000 people die each year as a consequence of addiction to cigarettes. More than 100,000 die annually of alcoholism. Deaths associated with illegal drugs, however, number approximately 20,000 each year. This is not to minimize the tragic and serious consequence of addiction to cocaine or heroin. These data, however, place into proper perspective the more significant problems associated with addiction to alcohol and/or tobacco.

They not only take their terrible toll, but they constitute the gateway to the use of illicit drugs.

Drugs impose an enormous economic burden. One recent study concludes that substance abuse costs the American taxpayers more than $160 billion per year in lost productivity, health care costs, work-related accidents, and crime. (John H. Osterlow and Charles E. Becker: "Chemical Dependency and Drug Testing in the Work Place," *The Western Journal of Medicine*, vol. 152, May 1990, pp. 506–13.)

Whether freedom is lost through personal physical addiction or from political decree, such painful enslavements evoke a deep yearning to be free from bondage once again. People denied the privileges of freedom of expression, freedom of religion, or freedom from addiction ultimately plead for the sweet perfume of the peaceful rose of freedom. But they must understand that this precious bloom must first be cultivated and then protected.

Indeed, the root of freedom is responsibility. The stem of freedom is discipline. The flower of freedom is vigilance.

Responsibility, discipline, and vigilance can be dispensed neither from the U.S. Treasury nor from private donations. This perception was shared by the Deputy Prime Minister of Czechoslovakia, with whom my associates and I spoke earlier this year. When we asked what specific aid could be rendered to Czechoslovakia's new democratic government, he replied: "We don't need material goods or technology. We need a new spirit. We need moral values. We need the Judeo-Christian ethic back in our curriculum. Please help us to make this a time of spiritual renewal for our nation."

In April of this year we met with the Minister of Education in the Republic of Estonia. We asked him a similar question. He replied that the Estonian economy is changing rapidly. He noted an urgent need to educate his people differently. He said: "There is much work to be done in rewriting our text books. We have the hope that religion can be taught in all of the schools and that the spirit of Christianity can be woven within the fabric of our curriculum."

As he made those remarks I thought of the irony that strong

forces in these United States are trying to eradicate all evidences of religion or piety from our public schools. Meanwhile, citizens in these European nations that have been so deprived of religious influence now feel the detrimental impact of that loss.

Leaders in Hungary and Poland have likewise expressed new hope for their future. These nations, now wishing to enter the land of economic prosperity, plead for a revival of religious ideals and individual responsibility.

Many in these countries of middle and eastern Europe feel a real sense of frustration. Their search for meaning in life, while never easy, has become more difficult as their political ideology has changed. Concepts they previously considered dependable have failed, leaving many of their people searching for standards that endure.

In news conferences and in other interviews, I have observed that these people hunger and thirst for knowledge regarding spiritual and moral values. Their eagerness for information is so great that it is often difficult to terminate those discussions. It is not easy for us to comprehend the degree of spiritual starvation the people suffer.

Libraries around the world bulge with books on how to make the transition from capitalism to communism. Yet I am not aware of comparable treatises on how to make the liberating leap from communism to capitalism. In February of this year we met with a cabinet-level official of the Republic of Romania. In essence he said: "I find myself as a leader in a government now liberated from the despotic dictatorship that I have known most of my life. Now we need a new constitution, but we don't know how to write one. Not only that, we don't know where to turn for help. Our libraries contain no information on this subject."

As we consider where and how help may be given, who will do it? Everyone talks about keeping alive the eternal flame of freedom, but few offer to pay the gas bill.

Where and how will these freedom-loving people learn to change from a top-down form of government to a bottom-up mode of administration? The most apparent source of help for these nations struggling in their new quest for democracy and freedom is here in America. Obvious questions are, *should* we help? And, *can* we help?

My answer—a resounding yes! Patterns of the past can be followed once again. President Woodrow Wilson helped Czechoslovakia's first president, Tomas Garrigue Masaryk, establish the Republic of Czechoslovakia on the same principles on which the United States of America had been founded. Masaryk's manuscripts, held by the U.S. Library of Congress, testify to that reality.

John Quincy Adams, when he was Secretary of State of the United States of America in 1821, made this statement: "Wherever the standard of freedom and independence has been or shall be unfurled, there will be America's heart, her benedictions, and her prayers. But she goes not abroad in search of monsters to destroy. She is the well-wisher to the freedom and independence of all." (Cited by Ken Adelman, *The American Enterprise*, Jan-Feb 1990, p. 24.)

President Joseph F. Smith once said: "[God's] hand has been over this nation, and it is his purpose and design to enlarge it, make it glorious . . . to the end that those who are kept in bondage and serfdom may be brought to the enjoyment of the fullest freedom and liberty of conscience possible for intelligent men to exercise in the earth." (*Gospel Doctrine*, [Salt Lake City: Deseret Book Co., 1939], p. 409.)

Our conscience, our compassion, and our commitment direct us to share what we have with neighbors in need. And we need not necessarily start with "big ticket" items. We can begin by relating precious divine law that defines the duty of government while yet preserving individual liberty. Heed a portion of that scripture:

> Religion is instituted of God; and . . . men are amenable to him, and to him only, for the exercise of it, unless their religious opinions prompt them to infringe upon the rights and liberties of others; but we do not believe that human law has a right to interfere in prescribing rules of worship to bind the consciences of men, nor dictate forms for public or private devotion; that the civil magistrate should restrain crime, but never control conscience; should punish guilt, but never suppress the freedom of the soul. (D&C 134:4.)

Along with the teaching of such divinely inspired doctrine, other affordable options might include the sharing of four blessings of freedom:

1. Technology
2. Democratic Rule of Law
3. An Example of Hope
4. Faith in God

1. TECHNOLOGY

We can transfer what some have called liberation technology—photocopiers, fax machines, computers, video recorders, and satellite dishes. Such technology helps to decentralize power and enlarge the capacity of an individual.

2. DEMOCRATIC RULE OF LAW

Americans with experience in the drafting of constitutions could work with the "James Madisons" of other countries to help fashion a legal framework that could effectively restrict central authority. They could teach how to divide powers between the executive, legislative, and judicial branches, and encourage federalism by granting local autonomy. The wise idea of deliberately building in tension between separate branches of government, with necessary checks and balances, constitutes a true safeguard of people's liberties.

The rule of law both in word and in practice is the strength and bulwark of any democracy. But correct statutes are only the beginning of rule by law. Laws must be conscientiously obeyed and impartially enforced by all, citizen and bureaucrat, tourist guide and policeman alike. The rule of law works in a democracy because its citizens adhere to a government of laws and act to see that the laws are evenly enforced. There must be shared respect as well as shared power. No individual is above or below the law.

3. An Example of Hope

Personal example is more eloquent than exhortation. There is a real difference between false freedom and true freedom. It is the difference between doing what we *wish* to do and doing what we *ought* to do. License to do wrong does not justify wrongdoing.

Even though most of us will not be called upon directly to help nations organize their newly found freedoms, all of us can participate by making certain the flame of freedom burns brightly and correctly within our own souls.

By example, we can show that political freedom provides personal freedom, and that personal freedom deserves to be safeguarded from surrender to pornography or to chemical compounds. We must have inner strength to protect personal freedom and preserve us from the yoke of bondage. Children of God cannot be weaklings. Surely, discipline is requisite to discipleship.

To develop self-discipline, we must confine our individual actions within the delimiting bounds prescribed by the law of the land, moral law, and divine law. When one's individual actions are sternly disciplined to conform within those limits, then the full exercise of one's freedom can be enjoyed. In a genuine democracy, there is obedience even to the unenforceable. This concept was so beautifully expressed by Katherine Lee Bates:

> America! America!
> God mend thine every flaw,
> Confirm thy soul in self-control,
> Thy *liberty* in *law*.
> ("America the Beautiful" *Hymns*,
> no. 338; emphasis added.)

4. Faith in God

Men and women can best honor one another by treating one another as brothers and sisters—all children of one Heavenly Father. He is our Creator. It is He who has made us free. Obedience to His law is essential to liberty. Faith in God is requisite to full freedom of the soul. Our founding fathers understood this well.

Now we are justifiably concerned because of indications of increasing hostility to religion in this country. Threats of litigation recently caused cancellation of prayers that have long been traditional at high school graduations. That we could so disregard Deity who gave us freedom is indeed a pitiful parody. We would do well to heed these words of President Wilford Woodruff:

> The God of Heaven, who created this earth and placed his children upon it, gave unto them a law whereby they might be exalted and saved in a kingdom of glory. . . . Whatever law anyone keeps, he is preserved by that law, and he receives whatever reward that law guarantees unto him. It is the will of God that all his children should obey the highest law, that they may receive the highest glory that is ordained for all immortal beings. But God has given all his children an agency, to choose what law they will keep. (*The Discourses of Wilford Woodruff*, ed. G. Homer Durham [Salt Lake City: Bookcraft, 1946], p. 10. See also D&C 88:34–39.)

Our Creator has granted to us the privilege of choice. But He also holds us accountable for our choices. Faith in God will inspire us to be responsible, disciplined, and vigilant in nurturing the sweet flower of freedom and in sharing it with neighbors near and far.

My closing quotation could best be a prayerful echo of these words of Samuel F. Smith:

> Our fathers' God, to thee,
> Author of liberty,
> To thee we sing;
> Long may our land be bright
> With freedom's holy light.
> Protect us by thy might,
> Great God, our King!
> ("My Country, 'Tis of Thee," *Hymns*, no. 339.)

I so pray in the name of Jesus Christ, amen.

He [George Washington] was, indeed, in every sense of the words, a wise, a good, and a great man.... It may truly be said, that never did nature and fortune combine more perfectly to make a man great, and to place him in the same constellation with whatever worthies have merited from man an everlasting remembrance. For his was the singular destiny and merit, of leading the armies of his country successfully through an arduous war, for the establishment of its independence; of conducting its councils through the birth of a government, new in its forms and principles, until it had settled down into a quiet and orderly train; and of scrupulously obeying the laws through the whole of his career, civil and military, of which the history of the world furnishes no other example.

—Thomas Jefferson

6

"First in War, First in Peace, First in the Hearts of His Countrymen"

Elder L. Tom Perry

We have witnessed this month a great celebration honoring the victorious heroes of the Gulf War. This stunning victory has again restored pride in the hearts of Americans. The victory was so rapid and so complete that once again there is little doubt of our being positioned in the world as the most powerful of nations.

Through the miracle of television, we had a front-row seat to watch the conflict. The deadly accuracy of our weapons today certainly has caused me to wonder what must be done to stop having their sights ever trained on human life again. War is such a waste of life, property, and wealth! If we could only devise some way to turn our energies and abilities towards blessing mankind rather than destroying him, how wonderful the beautiful world the Lord has created for us would be.

So tonight we salute our great armed forces for their tremendous victory, and the faith and confidence they have restored for us in the great country we are privileged to live in.

Address given 23 June 1991.

We begin today, in this community, this year's celebration of the birth of our nation. This is our 215th birthday celebration. For the last fifteen years we have been carrying on a bicentennial celebration of the birth of our nation. In 1976 we celebrated the signing of the Declaration of Independence. The Declaration of Independence is not just a birth certification for this nation—it is much more! It did not merely announce our separation from Great Britain, but it also contained a magnificent preamble that revolutionized the principles and practices of government.

Other revolutions had taken place, but they signaled only a change in the rule of men. The Declaration of Independence effected a change in principle. The Declaration gave to us a promise that we would be governed in a land of freedom.

In 1987 we celebrated the completion of the making of the Constitution. We celebrated the liberty we enjoy by virtue of a government established by the people when they ratified the Constitution. The Constitution was a fulfillment of the promised liberty granted to us in the Declaration of Independence. I like to think of the Declaration of Independence as a promise, and the Constitution as the fulfillment of that promise.

In 1988 we celebrated the ratification of the Constitution by New Hampshire, which was the ninth state to ratify. New Hampshire's action marked the two-thirds necessary for approval.

In 1990 we celebrated the ratification of the final state, Rhode Island. This completed the count of all thirteen states.

This year we celebrate the first ten amendments to the Constitution, entitled the Bill of Rights. Probably no debate was greater in the Constitutional Convention than that over the ratification of the Bill of Rights. Most believed that it was not necessary—that those rights were secured in the body of the Constitution.

Alexander Hamilton and others gave three reasons why the Bill of Rights was not necessary. *First:* the Constitution is a declaration of rights from beginning to end; nearly three hundred rights are pinpointed in the document itself. *Second:* under our limited form of government, with only twenty specific, enumerated powers granted to the federal government, there is absolutely no authority included to regulate or invade a citizen's freedom of religion, freedom of press, freedom of assembly, or freedom of petition. *Third:* there was a danger in making a list of individual rights, because under the law any right accidentally left off of the list might be presumed to be forfeited.

In spite of all this, however, the people insisted on a Bill of Rights. They feared from the bitter experiences of the past that the courts or government executives might somehow twist the meaning of certain words of the Constitution so as to deprive them of their rights, precisely as King George and his officers had done.

That is why George Mason, a leading patriot from Virginia, declared that he would rather have his right hand chopped off than to sign the Constitution without a Bill of Rights. It was on December 15, 1791, that the Bill of Rights was ratified, marking the first ten amendments to the Constitution.

The history of our Constitution since its writing in 1787 to the present is a history of being used as a model by nations of the world for their own constitutions. Except for six countries, every nation possessing a one-document constitution, or committed in principle to having one, invariably has followed the United States model. The United States Constitution is this nation's most important export.

The British statesman William Gladstone characterized the Constitution as "the most wonderful work ever struck off at a given time by the brain and purpose of man." And it has been so regarded abroad.

Ours is the oldest constitution in the world. Nearly two-thirds of the world's 160 national constitutions have been adopted or revised since 1970, and only fourteen predate World War II. The average nation has had two constitutions since the second World War. By these standards, the Constitution of the United States has proven to be remarkably durable.

As I review history I am always amazed at the power of leadership and the sacrifice required to be a good leader. This nation was truly endowed with great men as its founding fathers. Twenty-five centuries ago one of God's chosen prophets was told: "And insomuch as ye shall keep my commandments, ye shall prosper, and shall be led to a land of promise; yea, even a land which I have prepared for you; yea, a land which is choice above all other lands" (1 Nephi 2:20).

We are often reminded in holy writ that this is a promised land. Yet in His ultimate wisdom God did not limit His efforts to setting aside only a promised land, but also prepared certain leaders to come forth at specific times to implement His promises relative to this land.

> Now the Lord had shown unto me, Abraham, the intelligences that were organized before the world was; and among all of these there were many of the noble and great ones;
>
> And God saw these souls that they were good, and He stood in the midst of them, and He said: These I will make my rulers; for He stood among those that were spirits, and He saw that they were good. (Abraham 3:22–23.)

Again in the scriptures, even more explicit: "And for this purpose have I established the Constitution of this land, by the hands of wise men whom I raised up unto this very purpose, and redeemed the land by the shedding of blood" (D&C 101:80).

For these specific roles in life that have eternal consequences, even the best of plans would be for naught if it weren't for the required people to implement them. Some of the greatest and most noble spirits in heaven, men like Columbus, Governor Bradford, Samuel Adams, James Madison, Benjamin Franklin, and Abraham Lincoln were men driven with a keen sense of their unique mission from on high.

I want to single out one special man as we meet tonight, a man I believe to be one of the most noble and great men who have lived in this promised land: the father of our country, George Washington. His life is a testament of the hand of Providence in the founding of our country. George Washington was born on February 22, 1732, at Pope's Creek in the County of

Westmoreland, in the eastern part of Virginia, known as "the Tide Water Country."

During the early years between Washington's birth and the time he moved to Mount Vernon in 1748, very little is known. However, it may be safely stated that George Washington's character was forged near the home fireplace by a strong mother, an industrious father, a considerate brother, and the helpful hand of Providence.

What can be said with considerable authority is that by the age of sixteen Washington had already developed traits and talents that would prove helpful to him throughout his life.

He developed a strong affinity for horses, a skill that would later prove essential for the tasks he would be asked to perform. During his limited formal school years his schoolmates would come in from the playground with disputes for him to solve. From that time until his death, he was almost always cast in the role of mediator, a role he performed masterfully.

At age thirteen he had written in his copybook, as well as engraving them upon his mind, the 110 Rules of Civility and Decent Behavior. The following are some good examples:

- Let your conversation be without malice or envy, for 'tis a sign of a tractable and commendable nature: and in all causes of passion admit reason to govern.
- Go not thither, where you know not, whether you shall be welcome or not. Give not advice without being asked and when desired do it briefly.
- Undertake not what you cannot perform but be careful to keep your promise.
- Be not tedious in discourse, make not many digressions, or repeat often the same manner of discourse.
- Speak not evil of the absent, for it is unjust.
- When you speak of God or his attributes, let it be seriously and with reverence. Honor and obey your natural parents altho they be poor.
- Let your recreations be manful, not sinful.
- Labor to keep alive in your breast that little spark of celestial fire called conscience.

In his schooling he loved mathematics, which eventually led him to the study of surveying, a very important fact in his destiny.

In 1751 George received his first military appointment as assistant adjutant general for the Northern District of Virginia, with the rank of major. While in this position, he received additional training and responsibility that would prepare him for his next assignment in life.

During 1752–53, the French had been busily involved in expanding their territorial claims in the Ohio Valley and elsewhere on the Western frontier. At the same time they were becoming more hostile and were gathering their military forces to arouse the Indians against the British. In response to a request from England, Governor Dinwiddie was anxious to get a letter to the commandant of the French forces to warn them off. This was a mission of great difficulty and danger, an expedition of more than five hundred miles each way, much of it through hostile country. The first messenger selected had failed to accomplish the mission, so George Washington was selected. His being just 21 years of age and being given such a serious responsibility speaks volumes on the high esteem in which he was held by the leaders of the colonies.

On October 30, 1753, he set out on his first military mission, one that would tax all his skills and talents to the fullest. Before his small group arrived at their destination, Fort Boeuf, winter had arrived with all its fury. After delivering his message to the French commandant, they started back for Williamsburg. However, before they had traveled far they gave up riding their horses because of the deep snow and the poor condition of their horses. Leaving the others, Mr. Gist and Major Washington started the long walk back to Williamsburg.

After passing a town called Murdering Town, they met some Indians who had laid in wait for them. While stalking them, one Indian turned around and fired almost point blank at Washington and Gist, but fortunately missed. The next day they arrived at the Allegheny River. They had expected it to be frozen, but unfortunately it wasn't; so they were forced to spend the day building a raft for the crossing.

It is interesting to note that Providence was again protecting Washington: first, when the Indian fired almost point blank and missed him, and second, in spite of the fact that Washington fell into the river while making the crossing on the raft, he did not get frozen hands and toes, as Gist did.

They had traveled through rain, deep snow, perils of flood and starvation, and hostile Indians; and they successfully pushed their way back to Williamsburg. It is amazing that they had traveled the last five hundred miles in twenty-one days through pathless forests, flooded rivers, ice, and snow—all on foot. In recognition of his service on this expedition to the Ohio, Major Washington was promoted to lieutenant colonel in the Virginia Regiment.

Early the next year Washington was sent to the Ohio Valley to build a fort at the forks of the Ohio. He was placed second in command and led a small party of 160 troops. They arrived at Great Meadow on May 24, 1754. The troops were "green," poorly trained and equipped. With this small force he was to engage a French and Indian force many times larger, better trained and equipped. Although they had been instructed to build a fort at the forks, the French had already taken possession of the Ohio Company's fort. As a result, he built Fort Necessity, a small fort in the middle of a meadow about forty miles from the French fort.

On May 28, 1754, he was apprised that French soldiers and Indians were in the vicinity. After a long night of searching, they found the French and Indians and a skirmish took place in which eleven of the enemy were killed and twenty-one captured. This particular engagement actually started the French and Indian War.

It is interesting to note that all through this encampment of Washington's troops he insisted that they hold daily prayers and forbade them to swear.

From July to November, Washington attempted to maintain the front against terrible odds. Because of the worsening Ohio Valley problem, Governor Dinwiddie wrote to England requesting help. On February 14, 1755, General Braddock arrived in Alexandria, Virginia, with over two thousand troops. Two months later he requested that George Washington accompany him on a trek into the wilderness. Unfortunately, the general did not listen to Washington's advice on how the French and Indians fought—a mistake that would later cost him his life.

On July 9, 1755, General Braddock's troops marched into a small valley surrounded by tall grass, brush, and trees (about seven miles from Pittsburgh). As soon as most of his advance troops entered the valley, the French and Indians who had lain in ambush opened fire, killing 456 soldiers and wounding 422. During this engagement, General Braddock had five horses shot out from under him and received wounds that resulted in his death three days later. George Washington had two horses shot out from under him and received four bullet holes in his jacket. Both men showed extraordinary courage during this fierce battle.

It was said of George Washington by a friend who witnessed the battle: "I expected every moment to see him fall. His duty and situation exposed him to every danger. Nothing but the superintending care of Providence could have saved him from the fate of all around him."

He was appointed the Virginia Commander-in-Chief, and was in charge of maintaining a 350-mile frontier in the Ohio Valley. He was expected to protect the settlers and stem the tide of the French and Indians in the area.

Fifteen years after this battle, while exploring lands near the battle site, he was visited by an old Indian chief—the same one who had led the Indians in the ambush. He had heard that Colonel Washington was in their area and had come to pay him homage. The chief addressed Washington through an interpreter. He said:

> I am a chief and a ruler over my tribes. My influence extends to the waters of the great lakes, and to the far blue mountains. I have traveled a long and weary path, that I might see the young warrior of the great battle. It was on the day when the white man's blood mixed with the streams of our forest, that I first beheld this chief. I called to my young men and said, 'Mark yon tall and daring warrior? He is not of the red coat tribe—he

hath an Indian's wisdom, and his warriors fight as we do—he, himself, is alone exposed. Quick, let your aim be certain, and he dies.' Our rifles were leveled, rifles which, but for him, knew not how to miss. 'Twas all in vain, a power mightier far than we, shielded him from harm. He cannot die in battle. I am old, and soon shall be gathered to the great council fire of my fathers in the land of shades, but ere I go, there is something bids me speak in the voice of prophecy. Listen!

The Great Spirit protects that man, and guides his destinies—he will become the chief of nations, and a people yet unborn will hail him as the founder of a mighty empire. (*Recollections and Private Memoirs of Washington*, by George Washington Parke Custis, 1860, p. 303.)

Colonel Washington was elected to the House of Burgesses (the Virginia legislative group) while he was in the Ohio Valley, and he entered that body during January of 1759, where he served as a member for fifteen years.

Between 1759 and 1774 Colonel Washington enjoyed the life of a farmer, his first real love. He maintained a continued involvement in religious and civic projects.

In 1774 he was selected to attend the first Continental Congress in Carpenter's Hall in Philadelphia. It was attended by the most influential men in the colonies. During the prayer offered at the beginning of the session, George Washington was the only member who knelt down.

Patrick Henry was asked whom he thought was the greatest man in the Congress. He replied: "If you speak of eloquence, Mr. Rutledge of South Carolina is by far the greatest orator; but if you speak of solid information and sound judgment, Colonel Washington was unquestionably the greatest man on the floor." (Lossing, Vol. 2, p. 669.)

Washington may have been the most notable of the founding fathers, but an earnest study of history surely testifies to the fact that the Lord has blessed this nation with great and powerful leadership from the very beginning. How blessed we are to live under the banner of freedom! As we relish the sweetness of victory in our latest conflict, let us never forget that with victory also comes the burden of leadership for the future.

Many nations today are enjoying the privilege of newly found freedoms. Entire generations which have never known what it is to be free to worship, to speak, to print, or to assemble according to the dictates of their own conscience now have their freedom. They are struggling to find a way to ensure that these newly found freedoms and opportunities will never be lost again.

I cannot remember a time when the impact of righteous leadership was more desired by so many of the world's nations than it is today. They now know the power of our armed forces. Is this not a time to use this window of opportunity presently available to us, to let them know the power of our system of leadership and freedom? Is this not a time to let them see the power of our example, of faith, hope, integrity, morality, and industry, to be a beacon to all the world?

Even the military forces have discovered and altered leadership training. Recently I was invited to return to the San Diego Marine Corps Recruit Depot, where I received basic training during World War II. They have realized that, with the current tools of the military, a specially prepared marine is required. Drill instructors must now lead with inspiration and example rather than through abuse and foul language. Drugs are not tolerated—a onetime offense will cause the loss of marine status. Recruits are prohibited from using tobacco and alcohol during basic training, and are encouraged on Sunday to attend religious services of their choice, where values are taught. I was impressed with the new objectives to develop a higher-type leader.

Of course, we continue to need the dramatic leadership of the likes of Washington, Franklin, Madison, Jefferson, Lincoln, and so many others. But in addition we need to show that it really works all the way down to the grass roots level. We need a real demonstration of leadership in our homes, our neighborhoods, our schools, our communities, and our state.

Mediation is proper between two alternatives that are both right, but compromise is totally unjustified when it is between a right and a wrong course of action. Our founding fathers were inspired to deliver to this nation a conscience, a standard of values, with which we have been richly blessed in over two hundred years of our history.

Though times and seasons do change, foundation principles do not. This season of celebration and commemoration is an ideal time to focus on our glorious history and make firm resolve that we will not be just spectators but also participants in ensuring that the foundation principles are being preserved, safeguarded, and practiced in our own lives, with leadership, enthusiasm, and spirit.

Our faith, our conscience, our integrity, our industry, our hope—these can never be allowed to erode to mediocrity. Literally, the hope of those nations with the newly found freedoms depends on our continued example that this system works even better now than it has over our two hundred years of history.

May we prove by the way we live that we are just as powerful in the pursuit of peace and righteousness as our armed forces have proved to be in waging war. God grant that our leadership in this troubled world will be strong, bold, courageous, enthusiastic in defense of our foundation principles as an example to all mankind, who desire the blessings of freedom. This is my humble prayer in the name of our Lord and Savior, Jesus Christ. Amen.

Statesmen . . . may plan and speculate for liberty, but it is religion and morality alone which can establish the principles upon which freedom can securely stand.

—John Adams

7

Religion in a Free Society
ELDER M. RUSSELL BALLARD

Two hundred sixteen years ago the Continental Congress adopted the Declaration of Independence. Of that event John Adams said: "I am apt to believe that it will be celebrated by succeeding generations as the great anniversary festival. It ought to be commemorated as the day of deliverance by solemn acts of devotion to God Almighty. It ought to be solemnized with pomp and parade, with shows, games, sports, guns, bells, bonfires, and illuminations from one end of this continent to the other, from this time forward forevermore" (The Second Letter to Abigail Adams, July 3, 1776). This Provo Utah Freedom Festival surely fits John Adams's vision of our day.

At the outset please know that I do not represent myself to be an expert on religion in a free society, the subject of my talk tonight. I gratefully acknowledge the thoughtful suggestions of those who are knowledgeable and who have shared with me their thoughts, some of which I have included in what I will say.

I do, however, believe that I have some expertise as a father of our seven married children who have given to my wife and me the experience of being grandparents to their thirty-three children. It

---

Address given 5 July 1992.

is because of my love for them, and my deep concern that they and others like them be able to enjoy all of the privileges of religious liberty, that I express my thoughts this evening.

The breeze of freedom is blowing today with greater velocity throughout the world than perhaps at any other time in history. However, a gathering like this would still not be legally permissible in many places. We are meeting here on the Brigham Young University campus where The Church of Jesus Christ of Latter-day Saints freely supports this great institution.

Recently a group of religious and political leaders and scholars from all around the world met in Budapest, Hungary, to discuss the practical challenges faced by the former communist nations that are moving toward some form of religious liberty. The concept of religious freedom is revolutionary for many countries, and they are struggling with many potentially divisive issues: To what extent should public schools recognize and teach religion? How much should the state regulate a church's charitable activities? Should churches be exempted from general laws? To what degree should church and state be separated? Should there be an official state church?

Do those issues sound familiar? They should. Our founding fathers wrestled with them more than two hundred years ago, and they continue to be serious topics of discussion and debate to this very day.

The latitude we have for disagreement and discourse more than two hundred years after the United States Constitution and its Bill of Rights were enacted is a remarkable testimony to the enduring nature of those precious documents. The principles and philosophies upon which our constitutional law is based are not simply the result of the best efforts of a remarkable group of brilliant men. They were inspired by God, and the rights and privileges guaranteed in the Constitution are God-given, not man-derived. The freedom and independence afforded by the Constitution and the Bill of Rights are divine rights—sacred, essential, and inalienable. In section 98 of the Doctrine and Covenants the Lord indicates that "that law of the land which is constitutional, supporting that principle of freedom in maintaining rights and privileges, belongs to all mankind, and is justifiable before me" (D&C 98:5).

I focus my comments this evening on sixteen significant words found in the very First Amendment to the Constitution: "Congress shall make no law respecting an establishment of religion, or prohibiting the free exercise thereof."

These words are simple and direct. Their message and meaning appear to be clear. But through the years presidents, Congress, and the courts have interpreted them in so many different ways that many people today have no sense of the perspective upon which they were based.

Believe it or not, at one time the very notion of government had less to do with politics than with virtue. According to James Madison, often referred to as the father of the Constitution: "We have staked the whole future of American civilization not upon the power of the government—far from it. We have staked the future of all of our political institutions upon the capacity of each and all of us to govern ourselves according to the Ten Commandments of God." (Russ Walton, *Biblical Principles of Importance to Godly Christians* [New Hampshire: Plymouth Foundation, 1984], p. 361.)

George Washington agreed with his colleague James Madison. Said Washington: "Reason and experience both forbid us to expect that national morality can prevail in exclusion of religious principle" (James D. Richardson, *A Compilation of the Messages and Papers of the Presidents, 1789–1897*, published by authority of Congress, 1899, vol. 1, p. 220).

Nearly a hundred years later, Abraham Lincoln responded to a question about which side God was on during the Civil War with his profound insight: "I am not at all concerned about that, for I know that the Lord is always on the side of the right. But it is my constant anxiety and prayer that I and this nation should be on the Lord's side." (*Abraham Lincoln's Stories and Speeches*, J. B. McClure, ed. [Chicago: Rhodes and McClure Publishing Co., 1896], pp. 185–86.)

Madison, Washington, and Lincoln all understood that democracy cannot possibly flourish in a moral vacuum, and that organized religion plays an important role in preserving and maintaining public morality. Indeed, John Adams, another of America's founding fathers, insisted: "We have no government armed with power capable of contending with human passions unbridled by morality and religion" (John Adams, *The Works of John Adams, Second President of the United States,* Charles F. Adams, ed., 1854).

Yet that is precisely the position we find ourselves in today. Our government is succumbing to pressure to distance itself from God and religion. Consequently, the government is discovering that it is incapable of contending with people who are increasingly "unbridled by morality and religion." A simple constitutional prohibition of a state-sponsored church has evolved into court-ordered bans against (1) representations of the Ten Commandments on government buildings, (2) Christmas manger scenes on public property, and (3) prayer at public meetings. Instead of seeking the "national morality" based on "religious principle" that Washington spoke of, many are actively seeking a blind standard of legislative amorality, with a total exclusion of the mention of God in the public square.

Such a standard of religious exclusion is absolutely and unequivocally counter to the intention of those who designed our government. Do you think that mere chance placed the freedom to worship according to individual conscience among the first freedoms specified in the Bill of Rights—freedoms that are destined to flourish together or perish separately? The founding fathers understood this country's spiritual heritage. They frequently declared that God's hand was upon this nation, and that He was working through them to create what Chesterton once called "a nation with the soul of a church" (Richard John Newhaus, "A New Order for the Ages," a speech delivered to the Philadelphia Conference on Religious Freedom, May 30, 1991). While they were influenced by history and their accumulated knowledge, the single most influential reference source for their work on the Constitution was the Holy Bible. Doubtless they were familiar with the Lord's counsel to the children of Israel as they struggled to become a great nation:

> And it shall come to pass, if thou shalt hearken diligently unto the voice of the Lord thy God, to observe and do all his commandments which I command thee this day, that the Lord thy God will set thee on high above all nations of the earth:
>
> And all these blessings shall come on thee, and overtake thee, if thou shalt hearken unto the voice of the Lord thy God.
>
> Blessed shalt thou be in the city, and blessed shalt thou be in the field.
>
> Blessed shall be the fruit of thy body, and the fruit of thy ground, and the fruit of thy cattle, the increase of thy kine, and the flocks of thy sheep.
>
> Blessed shall be thy basket and thy store.
>
> Blessed shalt thou be when thou comest in, and blessed shalt thou be when thou goest out.
>
> The Lord shall cause thine enemies that rise up against thee to be smitten before thy face; they shall come out against thee one way, and flee before thee seven ways.
>
> The Lord shall command the blessing upon thee in thy storehouses, and in all that thou settest thine hand unto; and he shall bless thee in the land which the Lord thy God giveth thee.
>
> The Lord shall establish thee an holy people unto himself, as he hath sworn unto thee, if thou shalt keep the commandments of the Lord thy God, and walk in his ways. (Deuteronomy 28:1–9.)

In other words, that nation that keeps God's commandments and walks in His ways will prosper. The framers of our Constitution knew that, and they tried to lay a solid moral foundation for a society that could be so blessed. As they did so, perhaps they thought of Roger Williams and others like him who made a heroic fight for religious freedom.

Roger Williams, as you know, was one of the most courageous leaders of the Puritan movement. He began his ministry in England, where his zealous work to free the church from the influence of the king brought the wrath of the government upon him. Eventually he and his young wife were forced to flee to the New World. But instead of finding himself among like-minded reformers in

America, he encountered much of the same resistance and persecution until he established a new colony called Providence, in Rhode Island. Here America had its first taste of true religious freedom, and the success of the Providence colony convinced many that the concept tasted good.

The founding fathers very likely were aware of the experiences of Roger Williams and others when they wrote in the First Amendment that the government was not to impede the free exercise of religion. They wrote that the church and the state were to be separate, independent entities, not to eliminate morality and God's law but to make sure that the power of government could never be used to silence religious expression or to persecute religious practice. Once again quoting George Washington: "If I could have entertained the slightest apprehension that the Constitution, framed in the convention where I had the honor to preside, might possibly endanger the religious rights of any ecclesiastical society, certainly I would never have placed my signature to it" (*Maxims of Washington* [New York: D. Appleton and Company, 1894], pp. 370–71).

What would Washington have thought if he could have foreseen our day? Would he have signed the document?

I believe he would have been troubled to see a time when citizens are forbidden to pray in public meetings; when people claim that "you can't legislate morality," as if any law ever passed did not have at its heart some notion of right and wrong; when churches are called intruders when they speak out against public policy that is contrary to the commandments of God; when many people reject the correcting influence of churches if it infringes on daily living; when religion is accepted as a social organization but not as an integral part of national culture; when people bristle if churches speak in any forum except from the pulpit.

Indeed, some people now claim that the founding fathers' worst fear in connection with religion has been realized; that we have, in fact, a state-sponsored religion in America today. This new religion, adopted by many, does not have an identifiable name, but it operates just like a church. It exists in the form of doctrines and beliefs, where morality is whatever a person wants it to be, and where freedom is derived from the ideas of man and not from the laws of God. Many people adhere to this concept of morality with religious zeal and fervor, and courts and legislatures tend to support it.

While you may think I am stretching the point a bit to say that amorality could be a new state-sponsored religion, I believe you would agree that we do not have to look far to find horrifying evidence of rampant immorality that is permitted if not encouraged by our laws. From the plague of pornography to the devastation caused by addiction to drugs, illicit sex, and gambling, wickedness rears its ugly head everywhere, often gaining its foothold in society by invoking the powers of constitutional privilege.

We see a sad reality of contemporary life when many of the same people who defend the right of a pornographer to distribute exploitive films and photos would deny freedom of expression to people of faith because of an alleged fear of what might happen from religious influence on government or public meetings. While much of society has allowed gambling to wash over its communities, leaving broken families and individuals in its soul-destroying wake, it reserves its harshest ridicule for those who advocate obedience to God's commandments and to uniform, inspired standards of right and wrong.

As M.J. Sobran recently wrote, "A religious conviction is now a second-class conviction, expected to step deferentially to the back of the secular bus, and not to get uppity about it" (M.J. Sobran, *Human Life Review*, Summer 1978, pp. 58–59).

There are probably many reasons for the change in public attitudes toward religion. Certainly we've had too many wolves posing as shepherds, prompting a natural skepticism toward any who profess to represent God on earth. Of course the news media, which rarely report on the good things churches are doing in the world, almost never miss an opportunity to tell people when active church members do wrong. We read about crimes that are committed by former Sunday School teachers, ministers, or missionaries. But when was the last time you read that a crime was committed by someone who hasn't stepped inside a church in forty years?

For that matter, when was the last time you saw religion or people of faith portrayed positively in any film or television program? For the most part Hollywood's attitude toward religion is typified by the expression of cartoon character Bart Simpson, whose meal-time grace consisted of these words: "Dear God, we pay for all this stuff ourselves, so thanks for nothing." Can you imagine how embarrassed and disappointed our founding fathers would be to know of the blasphemous disregard that many of those of the media have for God our Eternal Father. In fact, noted film critic Michael Medved accuses Hollywood of a deliberate attempt to undermine organized religion. According to Medved, "A war against standards leads logically and inevitably to hostility to religion, because it is religious faith that provides the ultimate basis for all standards" (Michael Medved, "Popular Culture and the War Against Standards," a speech delivered at Hillsdale College November 18, 1990).

Organized religion finds itself increasingly on the defensive. Not only are people questioning the right of the church—*any* church—to be involved in matters of public policy, but some are even beginning to wonder whether the church is entitled to exert any kind of meaningful influence in people's lives. As one churchgoer recently said on a radio talk show: "I think the world of my minister—as long as he doesn't try to tell me how to live my life."

Is it any wonder, then, that religion now finds itself under attack in legislative assemblies and in the courts? In fact, the United States Supreme Court recently discontinued the time-honored judicial standard that gave considerable legal latitude to the free exercise of religion. Allowing people of faith to practice their religion free from the burdening effects of public policy is, according to the court, "a luxury that can no longer be afforded." While the justices acknowledged that the ruling would "place at a relative disadvantage those religious practices that are not widely engaged in," they said it was "an unavoidable consequence of a democratic government" (*Oregon Employment Division v. Smith*, 1990).

I do not promote the religious practice that was in question in that case but I am concerned with the long-term implications of the decision. Wherever religious groups are in the minority and are not considered part of the mainline religious community, the potential for state intrusion upon their religious practices is real. With legislative bodies responding most often to the will of the majority, the free exercise of religion by minority faith groups is in peril.

The Religious Freedom Restoration Act (HR 2797) is presently before Congress. This important piece of legislation is designed to restore the protections for religious freedom that existed before this recent Supreme Court decision placed those protections in jeopardy. Because the Religious Freedom Restoration Act is necessary for the preservation of the free exercise of religion, it demands our support.

The constitutional provisions relating to government and religion were not intended to control the religious rights of people. Rather, they were intended to expand them and eliminate the fear of government intrusion. These provisions were meant to separate religion and government so that religion would be independent. The experiences of Roger Williams and other reformers provided our constitutional fathers with important facts to help them deal with the potential risks of a state religion corrupted by politics. Consequently, they drafted an article in the Bill of Rights to guarantee religious freedom from government as opposed to government freedom from religion.

In fact, the framers of the Constitution probably assumed that religious freedom would establish religion as a watchdog over government, and believed that free churches would inevitably stand and speak against immoral or corrupt legislation. To do so, all churches not only have the right to speak out on public moral issues but they also have the solemn obligation to do so. Religion represents society's conscience, and must speak out when government chooses a course that is contrary to the laws of God. To remove the influence of religion from public policy simply because some are uncomfortable with any degree of moral restraint is like the passenger on a sinking ship who removes his life jacket because it is restrictive and uncomfortable.

We live in a day of political and social unrest. People are beginning to understand that more money and new government programs do not solve the problems of disintegrating morality in our homes and communities. People in the land have a feeling that things are not right. Voters everywhere are looking for a great leader to come along and straighten everything out.

The buzz words *family values* are being incorporated in almost every politician's favorite thirty-second sound bite. But what does that phrase really mean? Whose values are we going to embrace: The values of politicians? The values the media tell us we should cherish? The values of special interest groups and organizations? The values of rank-and-file Americans, as determined by scientific survey? Obviously, it would not be politically expedient to say that the values that our founding fathers drew upon are eternal, unchanging values. But that is a fact. The values that made us great are, in reality, the commandments of God. They provide the foundation upon which our republic was built. And if American democracy seems shaky today, it's only because that foundation has been eroded and weakened under the guise of separation of church and state.

Now that I think about it, maybe Washington really *was* speaking of our day when he said, "If I could conceive that the general government might ever be so administered as to render the liberty of conscience insecure, no one would be more zealous than myself to establish effectual barriers against the horrors of spiritual tyranny and every species of religious persecution" (*Maxims of Washington* [New York: D. Appleton and Company, 1894], p. 371).

Samuel Adams, who is sometimes called the father of the American Revolution, wrote: "I thank God that I have lived to see my country independent and free. She may long enjoy her independence and freedom if she will. It depends upon her virtue." (Wells, *The Life of Samuel Adams*, 3:175.)

That means it depends on us. If we would maintain the independence and freedom the founding fathers intended, we must work to preserve and protect the moral foundation upon which they built our government. We must stand boldly for righteousness and truth, and must defend the cause of honor, decency, and personal freedom espoused by Washington, Madison, Adams, Lincoln, and other leaders who acknowledged and loved God. Otherwise, we will find ourselves in the same predicament President Lincoln observed in 1863.

Said Lincoln: "We have grown in numbers, wealth and power as no other nation has ever grown. But we have forgotten God. We have forgotten the gracious hand which preserved us in peace and multiplied and enriched and strengthened us; and we have vainly imagined, in the deceitfulness of our hearts, that all these blessings were produced by some superior wisdom and virtue of our own. Intoxicated with unbroken success, we have become too self-sufficient to feel the necessity of redeeming and preserving grace, too proud to pray to the God that made us!" (Abraham Lincoln, A Proclamation *"to designate and set apart a day for National prayer and humiliation."*)

On this occasion of celebration, let us resolve to make our own families truly free by teaching them that God holds us all accountable. His laws are absolutes; breaking them brings unhappiness, even misery; keeping them brings joy, happiness, and the blessings of heaven. Let us teach our families and others the importance of moral responsibility based on the laws of God. Let us all resolve to listen to moral voices from churches and to those who speak in moral absolutes based on the commandments of God. Let us never support legislators that sponsor laws contrary to the laws of God.

The freedom we give thanks for tonight is at stake—for ourselves and for our posterity. No nation or people that rejects God or His commandments can prosper or find happiness. History and the scriptures are filled with examples of nations that rejected God. Let us be wise and remember the source of our blessings and not be timid or apologetic in sharing this knowlege with others.

There is no better place in this precious land of America than the great State of Utah for a people to embrace and declare that our trust is in God, and that we will look to His commandments and teachings for values that will fortify and give direction to society and our families. Only these values can ensure true happiness, lasting peace, and joy. May the leaders of the churches of America and the churches of Utah be allowed to help our nation and state to embrace the basic principles espoused and fought for by the founding fathers of this great nation. That is my prayer for all of us—but most especially for the future of my children and grandchildren and also yours. And I offer it humbly, and yet boldly, in the name of God's own Son, even Jesus Christ our Lord. Amen.

No free government, or the blessing of liberty, can be preserved to any people but by a firm adherence to justice, moderation, temperance, frugality, and virtue, and by frequent recurrence to fundamental principles.

—GEORGE MASON

8

America: "God Mend Thine Every Flaw"
Elder Neal A. Maxwell

Usually, and rightfully, we celebrate that dimension of patriotism which honors Americans who have fought militarily in defense of our freedoms—even going abroad to rescue the unfree and to make safe the distant shore.

Being privileged, almost within the month, to visit the 122-acre cemetery in France overlooking Omaha Beach, with its more than nine thousand sobering graves, was a moving experience. Families strolled the peaceful Omaha Beach that day. Gulls looped and swooped in serene flight. What a contrast to the thundering sounds of intense battle on that beach and on its overlooking bluffs, where, next June, it will be fifty years since D-Day at Normandy! What an unselfish thing it was for so many to give their lives so far from home and in behalf of so many others—whom they never even knew, but who nevertheless yearned for freedom!

Earlier there have also been, for me, tender and sobering visits back to Okinawa, where I participated briefly as an infantryman in that World War II campaign, and heard, firsthand, what

---

Address given 4 July 1993.

General MacArthur called "the strange, mournful mutter of the battlefield." (Army General Douglas MacArthur. Address accepting Sylvanus Thayer Award, West Point, 12 May 1962.) For me, therefore, this traditional dimension of patriotism is particularly and understandably touching and impressive. Yet it is only one important dimension of patriotism, for there are other expressions of patriotism that beckon us.

No attempt will be made tonight to exaggerate the virtues of America's past or to exaggerate the flaws of its present. Even so, reflecting on that special patriotic hymn, "America the Beautiful," provides so much to ponder! Given America's present circumstances, certain of the hymn's lyric phrases are actually haunting.

As we sing, for instance, of a "patriot dream that sees beyond the years," it reminds us of the special perspective that patriotism possesses. True patriotism takes a long view of this nation's needs. For instance, what does this reminding lyric tell us about our consistent and collective refusal, regardless of party, to face America's mounting national debt and our destabilizing budget deficits? The national debt increases one *billion* dollars every 24 hours—or in other words, during the few minutes I occupy this pulpit, America's national debt will grow by $694,444 *per minute*—approximately $21 million dollars! By this persistent lack of national resolve in our time we are robbing our children and grandchildren, however silently, of their economic freedom and future. We cannot seem to see beyond the political moment, let alone "beyond the years." Indeed, if certain conditions remain uncorrected in a lasting way, the "patriots' dream" may be replaced by some nightmares!

So it is that, whenever we talk about patriotism, the risks are that we will define it too narrowly. Moreover, no dimension of true patriotism is unworthy. Rather, no one portion comprises the whole of full patriotism. For instance, we would all quickly agree that patriotism is more than paying taxes. It is likewise more than voting. Yet it includes these—along with all the other unglamorous chores of citizenship. Patriotism requires public perspiration as well as an educated public . . . who can see "beyond the years."

Besides, the perspective of patriotism is vital because democracy and memory are not automatic partners, as Tocqueville observed: "Not only does democracy make every man forget his ancestors, but it hides his descendants and separates his contemporaries from him; it throws him back forever upon himself alone and threatens in the end to confine him entirely within the solitude of his own heart." (Alexis de Tocqueville, *Democracy in America*, as quoted in Andrew M. Scott, *Political Thought in America*, Rinehart & Co., Inc., 1959, p. 225.) Such loneliness and isolation can increase selfishness.

By contrast, James Wilson, one of America's founding fathers, urged delegates to the Constitutional Convention of 1787 to look beyond their own time and constituencies to the needs of generations yet unborn. They did, and all succeeding generations were blessed! Patriotism that sees "beyond the years" leaves legacies to rising generations instead of debt. It leaves clean turf, not the debris-strewn fields of a selfish society. Tolkien wisely counseled: "It is not our part to master all the tides of the world, but to do what is in us for the succour of those years wherein we are set, uprooting the evil in the fields that we know, so that those who live after may have clean earth to till. What weather they shall have is not ours to rule." (Gandolf in *The Return of the King*, by J.R.R. Tolkien. New York: Ballantine Books, 1965, p. 190.)

How are we doing with "those years wherein we are set"?

As we sing the words "confirm thy soul in self-control," what of our society's increasing lack of impulse control? So many people "act out" their impulses in so many inappropriate and destructive ways, including the neglect of families and children. More than we realize, our whole society really rests on the capacity of its citizens to give "obedience to the unenforceable." We do this by complying willingly with the law and behaving voluntarily according to time-tested standards. Such citizenship expresses a high form of volunteerism. In contrast, widespread and sustained lack of self-control, however, will bring either several external controls or anarchy. America's founders were determined to avoid both of those awful alternatives.

The lack of self-control, collectively and individually, adds to our debt, to America's devastating drug problem, and to our growing crime. The quality of self-control is best grown in healthy family gardens, yet so many families are failing. Healthy families are the first places in which we learn how to balance rights and responsibilities.

In "America the Beautiful" we also sing about establishing a "thoroughfare of freedom." Many of our streets, instead of being a "thoroughfare of freedom," are unsafe. Ironically, drugs and pornography often have staked out their own well-worn "thoroughfares" or corridors, and "free" zones. Surely it is one of the first duties of government to protect its citizens. Nevertheless, however beefed up, law enforcement cannot realistically be expected to compensate fully for widespread lack of individual self-control.

We rightly sing about how a "good" America should be crowned "with brotherhood." But instead of increasing brotherhood there is increasing separatism. There is even rising racism. Among our citizens there is also decreasing respect for each other. Engulfing gangs remind us soberingly of failing families and neighborhoods.

We sing, too, about how our "alabaster cities gleam, undimmed by human tears." Yet our cities don't gleam. Many are decaying, covered with graffiti. They are dimmed with human tears of desperation by those who feel left out of the American dream.

The challenges of urban decay actually threaten to overwhelm America. Thomas Jefferson was especially farseeing when he said that once people were piled upon people in big cities in America, then, as in Europe, America would have serious problems. We do!

Sorely needed, therefore, are wise expressions of patriotism that will improve the quality of life in our decaying cities.

We plead for God to "mend" America's "every flaw." But can we both acknowledge our flaws productively and believe in the Mender? God's blessings will depend upon our behavior. We can be "free from bondage, and from captivity," if we serve God (see Ether 2:12).

Being worthy of America's past and deserving God's blessings in the future are vital not only for America but also for the world. More hinges on what happens in America than we realize. It was so in the beginning as the Declaration of Independence was one of the special acts in human history. It not only affected the people of America but also spurred much of mankind. In an address in Independence Hall on February 22, 1861, Abraham Lincoln so noted, saying:

> I have often pondered over the dangers which were incurred by the men who assembled here and framed and adopted that Declaration. I have pondered over the toils that were endured by the officers and soldiers of the army who achieved that independence. I have often inquired of myself what great principle or idea it was that kept this Confederacy so long together. It was not the mere matter of separation of the colonies from the motherland, but that sentiment in the Declaration of Independence which *gave liberty not alone to the people of this country, but hope to all the world, for all future time*. It was that which gave promise that in due time the weights would be lifted from the shoulders of all men, and that all should have an *equal chance*. This is the sentiment embodied in the Declaration of Independence. (Emphasis added.)

America, with all its problems, is still a beacon. This beacon needs to shine more brightly today for the sake of all mankind in order to give, in Lincoln's words, "hope to all the world."

Whatever the dimension of patriotism, it requires that America have and maintain a spiritual core in order that our hopes are not in vain. Without this spiritual core, our liberties, our cities, our fiscal policies, and our brotherhood will finally falter and fail.

Virtue must, therefore, reside in the people as well as in the leaders. John Adams so cautioned: "Our constitution was made only for a moral and religious people. It is wholly inadequate to the government of any other." (In John R. Howe, Jr., *The Changing Political Thought of John Adams* [Princeton: Princeton University Press, 1966], p. 185.)

Unexciting as a prescription, nevertheless the best single way to improve the quality of life in America is to improve the quality of our own individual lives and our own neighborhoods. Otherwise, citizen failures to respect property or chastity—with all the consequences of those failures—cannot be corrected by mere legislation. Similarly, our neglect of the poor or of our civic duties cannot be corrected merely by Executive Orders.

Our inspired Constitution is wisely designed to protect us from our excess of power, but it can do little to protect us from excesses of appetite or from our indifference to great pinciples or institutions.

Any significant unraveling of the moral fiber of the American people, therefore, finally imperils the Constitution. The moral fabric of this society can become dangerously and relentlessly frayed as too few strands strain to hold us together. Hence shared patriotic, spiritual, and moral commitments within this nation's borders are as vital as defending those borders!

Therefore, while great leaders are needed, so also are informed and wise followers. John Stuart Mill counseled as follows:

> A people may prefer a free government, but if, from indolence, or carelessness, or cowardice, or want of public spirit, they are unequal to the exertions necessary for preserving it; if they will not fight for it when it is directly attacked; if they can be deluded by the artifices used to cheat them out of it; if by momentary discouragement, or temporary panic, or a fit of enthusiasm for an individual, they can be induced to lay their liberties at the feet even of a great man, or trust him with powers which enable him to subvert their institutions; in all these cases they are more or less unfit for liberty: and though it may be for their good to have had it even for a short time, they are unlikely long to enjoy it (*Considerations on Representative Government* [London: Parker, Son, and Bourn, West Strand., 1861], p. 6).

Aaron Wildavsky observed of the interaction of people and their leaders:

> Surely it would be surprising if the vices of politicians stemmed from the virtues of the people. What the people do to their

leaders must be at least as important as what the leaders do to them.

Citizenship and leadership are thus intertwined. So are individual morality and constitutional viability. So are rights and responsibilities.

Our various Constitutional freedoms are likewise irrevocably intertwined. For instance, President Rex Lee has observed of the interplay of certain freedoms: "Like the speech, press, and assembly guarantees, the free-exercise-of-religion clause deals directly with the protection of individual liberties, whereas the establishment clause is a structural provision, regulating institutional relationships between church and state. Moreover, speech and assembly are central to most religious activity." (Rex E. Lee, *A Lawyer Looks at the Constitution* [Provo: Brigham Young University Press, 1981], p. 135.)

As I move to the concluding portions, let us part the curtains of American history briefly. Doing so can permit our rich past to inspire our troubled present. This nation had an inspired and breathtakingly close passage in its founding. The initial success in founding this nation was not accidental; it was inspirational!

Catherine Drinker Bowen's book about the Constitutional Convention was appropriately called *Miracle at Philadelphia*. She wrote: "Miracles do not occur at random, nor was it the author of this book who said there was a miracle at Philadelphia in the year 1787. George Washington said it, and James Madison. They used the word in writing to their friends: Washington to Lafayette, Madison to Thomas Jefferson." (Catherine Drinker Bowen, *Miracle at Philadelphia* [Boston: Little, Brown, and Company, 1986], p. xi.)

Historian Barbara Tuchman called our founding fathers "the most remarkable generation of public men in the history of the United States or perhaps of any other nation" (Barbara W. Tuchman, *The March of Folly*, [New York: Alfred A. Knopf, 1984], p. 381). Tuchman said "it would be invaluable if we could know what produced this burst of talent from a base of only two and a half million inhabitants" (Tuchman, p. 383).

Some of us believe there was divine design associated with that "burst of talent," involving "wise men whom [God] raised up unto this very purpose" (D&C 101:80).

Of one of these, Washington, his prize-winning biographer, Flexner, has written: "In all history few men who possessed unassailable power have used that power so gently and self-effacingly for what their best instincts told them was the welfare of their neighbors and all mankind" (James Thomas Flexner, *Washington The Indispensable Man* [New York: Plume, 1984], p. xvi).

Power is most safe with those, like Washington, who are not in love with it.

The miracle of constitution writing at Philadelphia was soon followed by a second miracle, the miracle of Constitution ratification that ensued for ten months. Most of the same individuals "raised up" to write the Constitution also labored to help secure its ratification. But not all. Fighting ratification were prestigious and influential patriots like Samuel Adams, James Winthrop, George Mason, James Monroe—later to be the fifth president—and Patrick Henry!

In Pennsylvania, anti-federalists tried to stay away from the meeting in order to prevent the formation of the required quorum for ratification. Finally, two of the recalcitrant, anti-federalist assemblymen were dragged in and held in their seats until the business was successfully concluded. In December, after Pennsylvania ratified the Constitution, a mob attacked and beat James Wilson, the distinguished founding father quoted from earlier. Rhode Island did not even ratify until after the new government was functioning.

New Hampshire narrowly approved by 57 to 46, Virginia approved by a margin of only 10 out of 168. New York approved by the narrowest margin of 30 to 27.

Over two hundred years have passed since the twin miracles of writing and ratifying the Constitution. Surely America has not come thus far only to squander our precious liberties in license or our economic strengths in national indulgence!

In a real way, each generation of Americans has its chance to re-ratify the Constitution. We can do this by abiding by its principles and by leaving our own legacy to posterity; likewise, by both preserving our rights and filling our responsibilities. Otherwise, expressions of patriotism are no more than verbal veneration without actual emulation! Re-ratification will require statesmanship among both people and leaders. Statesmanship does not treat symptoms, but cures the underlying diseases. Our founding fathers did statesman-like work in 1776 and 1787. In our time, sadly, we seem preoccupied with treating symptoms, with quick fixes, and with getting by a little longer.

Yes, our Constitution has a marvelous system of checks and balances. But if uninspired individuals lack their own checks and balances, the inspired Constitution cannot correct that imbalance.

More remedies for our nation's ills are to be found in individual restraint than in restraining orders. More remedies are to be found inside our souls than inside our courts. Or, in families than in legislative bodies! There is more need for neighborly affection than for litigation in resolving local disputes. Yes, courts can adjudicate between citizens, but courts cannot supply one citizen with esteem for his fellow citizens.

Washington in his "Farewell Address" counseled: "Of all the dispositions and habits which lead to political prosperity, religion and morality are indispensable supports. In vain would that man claim the tribute of patriotism who should labor to subvert these great pillars of human happiness—the firmest props of the duties of men and citizens. The mere politician, equally with the pious man, ought to respect and cherish them. A volume could not trace all their connections with private and public felicity."

Earlier, in his first inaugural, Washington said: "There exists in the economy and course of nature an indissoluble union between virtue and happiness . . . we ought to be no less persuaded that the propitious smiles of Heaven can never be expected on a nation that disregards the eternal rules of order and right which Heaven itself has ordained."

Significantly, the Senate replied to Washington's Inaugural, saying: "We feel, sir, the force and acknowledge the justness of the observation that the foundations of our national policy should be lain in private morality. If individuals be not influenced by moral principles, it is in vain to look for public virtue." (Thomas G. West, "The Rule of Law in the Federalist," in *Saving the Revolution: The Federalist Papers and the American Founding*, ed. Charles R. Kesler [New York: The Free Press, 1987], 166–67.)

May I presume to speak for all of us as if to Washington on this July Fourth night, 1993, and say, with those senators, "We feel, Sir, the force and acknowledge the justness of your observations."

God bless America by helping us to mend our flaws! God bless all of you, in the name of Jesus Christ. Amen.

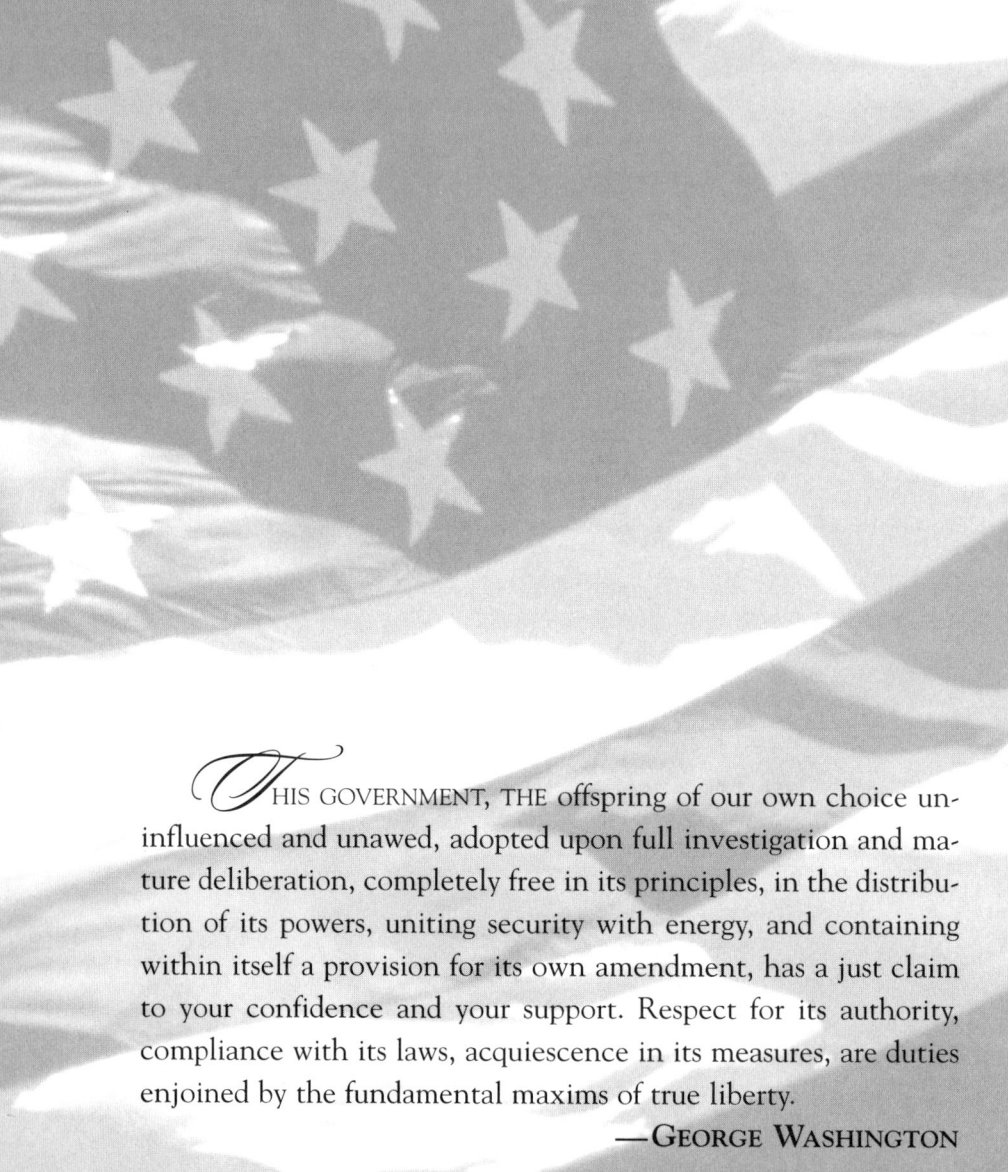

This government, the offspring of our own choice uninfluenced and unawed, adopted upon full investigation and mature deliberation, completely free in its principles, in the distribution of its powers, uniting security with energy, and containing within itself a provision for its own amendment, has a just claim to your confidence and your support. Respect for its authority, compliance with its laws, acquiescence in its measures, are duties enjoined by the fundamental maxims of true liberty.

—George Washington

9

Some Responsibilities of Citizenship
Elder Dallin H. Oaks

My dear brothers and sisters, I welcome this opportunity to speak to a Sabbath audience at America's Freedom Festival at Provo. This evening I wish to speak about some responsibilities of citizenship. My message consists of personal opinions and is not an expression of an official position.

About two months ago my wife, June, and I traveled from Brazil to Chile. En route we stopped at Iguacu, Brazil, to see the world's largest waterfall.

We approached the falls first from the downstream side. We were awed by the thunderous avalanche of water spilling over the rocky precipice and cascading over two hundred feet into the cataract below.

Later we walked through the state park several hundred feet above the falls. Here the wide Iguacu River flows serenely between low forested banks, with only an occasional ripple of white to mark a few boulders in its path. Here the river appears placid and inviting. As we looked downstream toward what we knew to be the location of the mighty falls, we could see nothing to warn

---

Address given 3 July 1994.

of their presence. From this point a boatman with no knowledge of the falls would have only a strange, distant roar to warn him of imminent disaster.

As I viewed this scene I thought of the circumstances of our nation. Prophetic voices have sounded warnings of a downfall ahead, of hazards that could deprive us of our freedom. Yet, as we look about us at this point, the flow of events seems serene, with only an occasional ripple. To see the danger we must rise above the immediate scene and tune our senses to identify changed conditions that threaten the future of our nation.

Responsibilities

A few months ago I received a letter from an old friend whose name and work should be familiar to all of us. Dr. Kenneth D. Wells is the founder of the famous Freedom Foundation at Valley Forge. Though now eighty-five years of age, this respected patriot, a convert to Mormonism, continues to do all that he can for the future of our nation. His letter, sent to many of his friends, cites the obvious malignancies that afflict our nation and concludes with these words:

> In my heart and mind and soul, I know only as our consciences turn us to "<u>Responsible Personal Conduct</u>" will the dream that is America have any chance of survival. (Kenneth D. Wells, letter of March 30, 1994.)

Some of the responsible personal conduct that is necessary to save America is the kind of conduct that is enforceable by law and legal process, but much of it can only be encouraged. In the end, many of our most important personal, family, civic, and church responsibilities are entirely voluntary. As Elder Neal A. Maxwell said in his address at this Freedom Festival last year, "Our whole society really rests on the capacity of its citizens to give 'obedience to the unenforceable.'"

At a time when most of our public discourse concerns *rights*, it may seem strange to speak of *responsibilities*. But a democratic republic needs patriotic citizens who are fulfilling their responsibilities as well as claiming their rights. No society is so secure that it can withstand continued demands for increases in citizen rights without producing corresponding increases in the fulfillment of citizen responsibilities. Responsibilities like honesty, respect for personal and property rights, self-reliance, and willingness to sacrifice for the common good are basic to the governance and preservation of our nation.

This evening I will speak of three fundamental responsibilities of citizenship in a democratic nation. In my lifetime each of these has been significantly compromised in theory and practice, and our nation has been significantly weakened in the process. One of these responsibilities has been undercut by the political Left. One has been undercut by the political Right. The third is being undercut by both the Left and the Right. These three fundamentals are the citizen responsibilities of (1) serving in the military, (2) paying taxes, and (3) participating in democratic government.

A Special Introduction for Church Members

Before I address these three responsibilities I will provide a short introduction that I believe is needed by some members of The Church of Jesus Christ of Latter-day Saints.

The twelfth Article of Faith commits Latter-day Saints to "being subject to kings, presidents, rulers, and magistrates," and to "obeying, honoring, and sustaining the law." This belief is not unique in Christendom. The apostle Paul told the early Christians to be "subject to principalities and powers, [and] to obey magistrates" (Titus 3:1; also see Romans 13:1). The Apostle Peter taught, "submit yourselves to every ordinance of man for the Lord's sake" (1 Peter 2:13).

This principle is embodied in the LDS Declaration of Belief in the Doctrine and Covenants, which reads: "We believe that all men are bound to sustain and uphold the respective governments in which they reside, while protected in their inherent and inalienable rights by the laws of such governments" (D&C 134:5).

Some Church members have questioned the meaning of the last clause. Some who have written me have claimed to be excused from their scriptural obligation to "sustain and uphold" their government because the government has not protected them in their inalienable rights. One letter included this statement: "What about the resistance movement during the conquering of Hitler's National Socialist war machine? I personally know of an LDS family who during World War II defied the Nazis by secretly saving lives of people (many of them were Jews) by hiding and transporting them by boat from Denmark to Sweden. Yet today they are still faithful members of the Church. Are they under condemnation for not obeying and sustaining the totalitarian government they were under?"

I feel sorry for persons whose knowledge of the relative actions of Nazi Germany and modern United States of America is so incomplete that they put these two governments in the same category in depriving their citizens of inalienable rights. We should all be able to recognize the difference between abuses that are individualized—and we surely have some of these in the United States today—and those that are deliberate government policy, as in Nazi Germany. A person who cannot tell the difference between a rat and a rhinoceros will be a poor source of advice on the control of animals.

At a clear and extreme level, violations of inalienable rights by a government might excuse citizens from the performance of some obligations of citizenship. But the history of Latter-day Saints' relations to their governments shows that any such exceptions would have to be far more extreme than anything we have experienced in this country.

Even when victimized by what they must surely have seen as very severe government oppressions and abridgments of freedom, the Mormon people and their leaders have remained loyal to their government and its laws. Think of the persecutions in Missouri, the expulsion from Nauvoo, and the repressions suffered in the Utah Territory. As long as a government provides aggrieved persons an opportunity to work to enlarge their freedoms and relieve their oppressions by legal and peaceful means, a Latter-day

Saint citizen's duty is to forego revolution and disobedience of law. Our doctrine commits us to work from within. Even an oppressive government is preferable to a state of lawlessness and anarchy in which the only ruling principle is force and every individual has a thousand oppressors. (See D&C 134:6.)

Church members who seek to use LDS doctrine as a basis for concluding that government infringements on inalienable rights have excused them from obeying the law seem to have forgotten the principle of following the prophets. Until the prophets invoke this principle, faithful members will also refrain from doing so. We remain committed to uphold our governments and to obey their laws.

MILITARY SERVICE AND TAXES

I come now to the first two fundamental citizen responsibilities that have been compromised in my lifetime in the United States: serving in the military and paying taxes.

Modern opponents of compulsory military service and of enforced payment of taxes have this common objection. Both claim that the government compulsion to do these unpopular things interferes with freedom. The issue, they say, is freedom versus slavery.

The problem with this argument is that it proves too much. It would take us back to the toothless Articles of Confederation from which our inspired Constitution rescued us. A government that cannot compel military service or a government that cannot compel the payment of taxes is not much of a government.

At root, these objections to government compulsion are objections to the whole idea of government. Such objections are contrary to Christian doctrine. Jesus did not preach sedition. He taught his followers to "render . . . unto Caesar the things which are Caesar's" (Matthew 22:21). His Apostles taught the same, as I have already noted.

Of course, there are legitimate technical objections to laws requiring military service and to certain tax laws, but these are objections to the terms of the law, not to the idea of compulsion. Technical objections should be presented in the forums provided by law.

During the Vietnam War, when I was a professor of law at The University of Chicago Law School, I knew some young men from the political Left who had a second type of objection to military service. They said they did not object to compulsory service in the military, but they did object to serving in the war in Vietnam because they opposed that war. The law, which must give equal protection to all citizens, did not recognize that kind of objection. Citizens cannot pick and choose which wars to support or which laws to observe. But there were many young men who asserted this objection, and there were times during the Vietnam War when the extent of draft evasion on this basis posed a serious problem for our nation.

Today there is a comparable objection to the payment of taxes, but this objection comes primarily from the political Right. People who object to some of the ways the government spends its tax revenues contend that they should not be forced to pay taxes to support activities they condemn. This picking and choosing which laws to support is the same legal approach the young men of the political Left used to try to avoid military service during the war in Vietnam.

One does not have to approve of all of the uses of military power nor all of the uses of tax revenues to see that taxpayers and young men of military age cannot resist compulsion on the basis of disagreements with some of the policies of the government that seeks to compel them. A government could not survive if the enforceable responsibilities of its citizens were divisible according to their individual preferences. We cannot be expected to welcome military service or to relish the payment of taxes, but we should recognize these as essential responsibilities of citizenship, even where we disagree with some of the actions of the government we support.

I know of no better commentary on taxes and big government than the consoling observation attributed to Will Rogers: "We're just lucky we're not gettin' all the government we're payin' for." I also enjoy most of the good-humored jokes about the Internal Revenue Service, which definitely does not qualify as everyone's favorite bureau. Someone said that the IRS has solved the problem of what to give to the man who already has everything: give him an audit!

So much for politics. I come now to objections based on some type of legal theory.

The first legal objection is that the basic law is unconstitutional. I do not remember such arguments being made against the draft law during the Vietnam War. However, for reasons I cannot explain, some persons are now arguing that the federal income tax is unconstitutional.

Church members involved in various forms of tax protest have sent me many legal memoranda that purport to justify their positions. For the first several years of my service as a General Authority, I did a good deal of personal research to evaluate these legal theories in view of the principles I had learned during a quarter of a century in the legal profession, including several years teaching tax law in a major law school. In not one single instance have I found any merit in the legal theories asserted as a basis for these tax protests. Yet some good people are still being misled by them, and their mistaken reliance on false theories is wreaking havoc with their financial prospects and even their spiritual lives.

A claim often made by protesting taxpayers is that the IRS is afraid to challenge them. Some who have written me have claimed that the merit of their position is evident in the fact that they have not filed a tax return for many years and nothing has happened to them. I received one such letter from a prominent tax protestor in Utah, and then, a few months later, read a press account of his beginning service of a long prison sentence in a federal penitentiary. The wheels of justice grind slowly, but exceedingly fine.

For many in this audience, the ultimate mortal authority on religious doctrines is the First Presidency of The Church of Jesus Christ of Latter-day Saints. Just last year, the Council of the First Presidency and Quorum of the Twelve gave this instruction:

> Church members in any nation are obligated by the twelfth article of faith to obey the tax laws of that nation (see also D&C 134:5).... A member who refuses to file a tax return, to pay required income taxes, or to comply with a final judgment in a tax case is in direct conflict with the law and with the teachings of the Church. (*Bulletin*, 1993–2, The Church of Jesus Christ of Latter-day Saints; also see *General Handbook of Instructions*, p. 11–2.)

There is nothing inappropriate in taking political action to reduce taxes or in pursuing well-founded court challenges to a particular application of the tax laws. In their 1993 statement, the Church leaders declared: "If a member disapproves of tax laws, he may attempt to have them changed by legislation or constitutional amendment, or, if he has a well-founded legal objection, he may challenge them in the courts." (Ibid.)

However, contrary to the position of some tax protestors, this statement provides no justification for a general and persistent failure to pay taxes or to refrain from filing tax returns. The courts that our Constitution and laws have established to rule on such matters have uniformly upheld the constitutionality of the federal income tax law and have regularly rejected assertions that wages and salaries are not taxable, that federal reserve notes do not count as income, and that individuals or businesses can elect not to comply with the income tax laws. As a result, failures to obey the income tax law that are based on these and similar theories must be regarded as actions without "a well-founded legal objection" and therefore unacceptable to persons committed to uphold and sustain the law.

THEORIES TO FREE CITIZENS FROM THE AUTHORITY OF GOVERNMENTS

Other variations on the avoidance of citizen responsibilities are the recent theories that purport to allow persons to free themselves from the authority of federal, state, or local governments.

The first of these theories was espoused by the so-called Township Movement. Under this theory, a person could execute some kind of document that would excuse him or her from any compulsory government authority other than the so-called township government this person had participated in electing. This theory purported to be based on common-law precedents going back to the earliest of times. Its defect is its ignoring or denying of the authority of the federal and state constitutions and laws adopted in this nation. The proponents of the Township Movement view history through a peephole that shows nothing but the subjects they desire. Their legal claims have no merit whatever.

The second theory that purports to allow a person to free himself or herself from paying taxes or being subject to other federal or state laws is the so-called state citizenship movement, which makes prominent reference to sovereign citizenship or common-law citizenship. This theory starts with a valid principle, the sovereignty of the people, but it misapplies that principle and reaches an erroneous conclusion.

One of the most important of the great fundamentals of our inspired Constitution is the principle that the sovereign power is in the people, not in a state or nation just because it has the power that comes from force of arms. Along with many other religious people, Latter-day Saints affirm that God gave the power to the people, and the people consented to a Constitution that delegated certain powers to the federal and state governments and reserved the rest to the people.

However, it does not follow from this principle that each citizen is free to determine which laws he will obey or that one or more citizens are free to redefine the concept of sovereignty. That would result in anarchy, a system in which the only source of power is the sword. In that system, no person is free. The United States Constitution and the constitutions of the several states have defined the powers citizens have granted to their governments, the procedures for amending those grants, and the means by which controversies over the exercise of those powers can be resolved.

Now to the theory of state or sovereign or common-law citizenship. A knowledgeable proponent of this theory, whose recent, long letter to me purported to be representative of large numbers of adherents in California and across the nation, some of whom are members of my church, gave this description of the theory (letter of Mar. 15, 1994): The 1783 Treaty of Paris (which concluded the Revolutionary War) granted sovereignty to the people of the thirteen colonies. The sovereign people of these colonies (later states) had no national citizenship. There was no national citizenship in the United States until 1868. The citizenship granted by the Fourteenth Amendment in 1868 gives national citizens only "subject status," not sovereignty. As a result, there are different classes of citizenship in the United States today, depending upon whether one's citizenship is based on the inferior status conferred by the Fourteenth Amendment or on the inherent sovereign citizenship that devolved upon residents of the various states as a result of the 1783 Treaty of Paris.

There are four major problems with this theory. *First*, the Treaty of Paris did not grant sovereignty to the citizens of the thirteen colonies. It is a treaty between "two countries," Great Britain and the United States of America. The treaty acknowledges the independence of the thirteen "states," as it calls them, but it refers to them collectively as "the United States of America." Moreover, the treaty was ratified by the Continental Congress, not by the legislatures of the thirteen states.

Second, the theory of state citizenship ignores the effect of the United States Constitution, which was ratified five years after the Treaty of Paris. That constitution established an entirely new relationship between the states and the national government, and the citizens of the states and the nation ratified that relationship by the procedures they had specified.

Third, the argument that there was only state citizenship prior to the Fourteenth Amendment ignores over 75 years of congressional and judicial action defining the separate incidence of federal and state citizenship. (See James H. Kettner, *The Development of American Citizenship 1608–1870* [Univ. No. Carolina Press, 1978].)

Finally, the asserted theory also ignores the effect of the Fourteenth Amendment of the United States Constitution, which defines national citizenship for all citizens of this nation and its constituent states.

Persons who believe in the so-called "state citizenship movement" are encouraged to sign and publicly file three "legal documents," including a "Declaration of Citizenship and Status as a Common-law Citizen." These documents are supposed to revoke the signers' national citizenship and free them from tax and other legal obligations to the United States. Considering the care with which these meaningless documents are drafted and executed, I am reminded of a wise aphorism: "A task not worth doing at all is not worth doing well."

One recent letter to Church headquarters even suggested that such persons have no legal need to get a marriage license, and therefore should be able to have a temple marriage without one. Persons who claim the right to pick and choose which laws of the land they will observe are not far from claiming to choose which laws of God they must observe.

I feel sad that persons can be so misled. The wise will beware of teachings on the constitution that are based on peephole history and selective readings of historic documents. They should also beware of the related advice of persons who advocate private armies or the collection of heavy weapons or extraordinary quantities of private arms. Responsible citizenship has no shortcuts when the going gets tough—not draft avoidance, not tax evasion, and not eccentric theories that purport to free us from the obligation to be subject to the constitutions and laws of our states and our nation.

Participating in Democratic Government

The solution to many of the major problems in our nation is for more citizens to participate more actively and more effectively in democratic government, by their votes and by their letters and other communications to elected representatives. This fundamental responsibility of citizenship is a prerequisite for the perpetuation of freedom.

I will cite three major national problems that I believe would yield, long-term, to increased citizen participation.

1. *The budget deficit.* We know that our national government cannot continue indefinitely to spend more than it receives. If the citizen-voters of this nation continue to demand the current level of government expenditures that produces our deficits, then our citizen-taxpayers must accept the tax increases necessary to fund them. If we won't raise taxes, we should accept cuts in various expenditures. We cannot continue much longer to fund our current levels of government expenditures by increased borrowings.

This problem cannot be solved by the popular but superficial action of merely opposing all tax increases. It cannot be solved by the phony solution of proposing spending cuts on every government program except our various personal favorites. This familiar approach shatters working coalitions and imposes gridlock on progress toward reducing deficits. Citizen-taxpayers have endured the resulting government paralysis on deficit reduction for years, until we are about to drift over the fiscal falls from the effects of the national debt.

Citizen-voters should demand that our elected president and lawmakers act decisively and courageously to reduce the steeply increasing debt we are leaving to our children and grandchildren and the progressively paralyzing proportion of current income our government must pay as interest on that debt.

2. *The allocation of power between federal and state governments.* For more than a half century, our national government has been acquiring additional powers by assuming functions previously left to state and local governments. This trend has now gone so far that the national government is beginning to direct what state and local governments must do and even how they must spend their limited revenues. This trend must be stopped and reversed, or we will cease to be the federal republic established in our inspired Constitution.

I am glad that some of our state governors are challenging this trend. I welcome their leadership in objecting to congressional action that commandeers the legislative and regulatory processes of the states to carry out federal directives not financed by the federal government. I hope many citizens will respond to such leadership and work to assure that state governments and their subsidiary local governments will continue to have a strong and effective role in our nation.

It is imperative that state governments have the power and the fiscal resources to respond to local needs and to capitalize on local strengths. That is the essence of federalism. But if federalism is to work, state governments must be willing to move against local and regional problems, such as clean air and water, and not wait for every such initiative to come from the national government. The current imbalance between the national and the state governments is just as much a product of state inaction as it is of national overreaching.

The balance I advocate between national and state powers is mandated by the Tenth Amendment, which provides: "The powers not delegated to the United States by the Constitution, nor prohibited by it to the States, are reserved to the States respectively, or to the people."

The Tenth Amendment's reference to powers delegated to the United States by the Constitution leads me to a third subject of concern.

3. *We need to reestablish the constitutional principle that our federal government is a government of limited powers.* A government of limited powers was the central premise of constitutional law during the first century and a half of our nation's history. Constitutional discussions of that period generally focused not on questions of individual rights but on whether the Constitution granted power to authorize the government activity that was challenged.

In the aftermath of the Great Depression and World War II, this traditional assumption of limited federal government powers was gradually displaced by the idea that the national government presumably possesses law-making powers except to the extent prohibited by some person's defined constitutional right. As a result of this change, current legal and political debate over excessive or undesirable government regulation tends to focus on whether some individual constitutional rights have been invaded.

> In effect, . . . [this] shifts the burden of proof concerning the appropriateness of an exercise of government power from the state to the right holder. New assertions of government power are no longer suspect. Where no constitutional right is clearly available as a shield, new assertions of government authority meet passive acquiescence.
> . . . [We] need to revitalize the old wisdom that the protection of individual freedom often requires limiting government powers in ways that go beyond merely vindicating individual rights. We must cage the lion as well as arm the spectators. (W. Cole Durham, Jr., and Dallin H. Oaks, "Constitutional Protections for Independent Higher Education: Limited Powers and Institutional Rights," in *Church and College: a Vital Partnership*, vol. 3, *Accountability*, pp. 71–72 [National Congress on Church-related Colleges and Universities, Austin College, Sherman, Texas, 1980].)

Because it requires changing deeply held assumptions and fundamental constitutional interpretations, this third major problem will be the most difficult to resolve. But it is also the most important. In the pantheon of ideas in our divinely inspired Constitution, the idea that the government is limited to the powers expressly and impliedly conferred by the Constitution is second only to the principle that the people are sovereign.

I have advocated greater citizen participation to resolve three major problems: (1) our massive and increasing national deficits, (2) the need for states to reacquire powers and initiatives taken away by the federal government, and (3) the need to reestablish the principle that the federal government is a government of limited powers.

A Caution on Citizen Participation in Single-Interest Groups

Even as I call for greater citizen participation to resolve national problems, I must voice one caution about citizen participation. I believe that citizen participation in single-interest groups is actually weakening representative government.

Interest groups are inevitable and desirable in a democratic government. For example, political parties are interest groups, comprised of persons with many different specific interests. Political parties blunt the extreme effects of their constituent special-interest groups as those parties compel the internal compromises necessary to mold their constituencies into a working coalition. In contrast, single-interest groups confront government directly with uncompromised demands on a narrow spectrum of issues. These groups are so specialized that they lack the perspective to move against the large problems, and they also lack the incentive to make the pragmatic compromises that are the enabling force of democratic government in a pluralistic society.

Some of the most powerful influences in the government of our nation in this last decade of the twentieth century are the multitude of single-interest groups. Whether the subject is gun control, medical care, criminal punishment, welfare reform, government aid to this or that, or whatever, these single-interest groups are a formidable force in lobbying, in fund-raising, and in citizen involvement. None of these groups is powerful enough to steer the ship of state by itself, but many have sufficient power to prevent the vessel from being steered toward the solution of more general problems. In other words, single-interest groups are not able to lead toward the solution of general problems, but they are commonly able to block such solutions. And what they block can be the solution of the large general problems that affect the entire body politic, such as deficit-spending or others I have mentioned.

Contrast the example of the founding fathers. The United States Constitution could never have been drafted or ratified if each of the delegates to the convention had focused on his own special interest and had demanded full satisfaction as the price of his support. The history of our Constitution is replete with examples of farsighted statesmen who were willing to support a document that failed to implement many of their personal preferences. For example, influential Thomas Jefferson, who did not serve as a delegate because he was in Paris negotiating a treaty, felt strongly that a bill of rights should have been included in the original Constitution. But Jefferson still supported the Constitution because he felt it was the best available at the time. Benjamin Franklin described that same approach when he said: "The opinions I have had of its errors, I sacrifice to the public good." (*Notes of the Debates in the Federal Convention of 1787, Reported by James Madison*, p. 653.)

In other words, we must not go into blocking tactics when a representative body fails to satisfy us fully on our favorite special interest. We should not expect all our personal preferences in government action that must represent a consensus. Americans are well advised to support the best that can be obtained in the circumstances that prevail. The conduct of the most important business of our nation must not be held hostage to the fulfillment of every preference of every powerful special-interest group. In a democracy and a society committed to pluralism, we must be willing to compromise on public policies from year to year, and then apply ourselves diligently to the tiresome tasks of education and persuasion and lobbying in order to obtain our way to an increasing extent as we win agreement from our fellow citizens.

One aspect of our current single-interest politics that is a special worry to me is the fear that many Americans will have their only political activity through a particular single-interest group. If most who are politically active see the political process and the future of our country only through the keyhole of one particular special interest, where will we get the vision and perspective necessary to guide the ship of state on the largest and most important issues that confront us? Responsible citizenship requires that we see our venture in self-government in broader terms than merely through the lens of one special interest, however important and however strongly felt.

I do not suggest that anyone refrain from pressing whatever special interest is important to him or her. But I am bold enough to suggest that no person should limit his or her political activity to a single subject. For example, a person who strongly supports one special interest should also make a conscious effort to help resolve larger government problems on which that person can unite with some of the same persons who are the opposition in the area of special interest. There are plenty of areas for general citizen participation on subjects not usually classified as single interests. In addition to deficit reduction and the other topics mentioned earlier, I would include education policy, transportation policy, environmental concerns, and the necessarily broad-based activities of political parties at the local, state, and national levels.

General citizen cooperative action that transcends special interests can also be achieved through the multitude of private volunteer organizations that are unique and so important to our nation. A partial list of these will include activities familiar to everyone in this audience.

1. The celebration of citizenship, patriotism, and national holidays and values, such as hundreds of volunteers do so well in this Freedom Festival.

2. Volunteer work in hospitals, museums, public radio and television, and various arts organizations such as symphony, ballet, and theater.

3. Assisting the great system of private education that is unique to the United States of America, at the elementary, secondary, and college/university level.

4. Helping to clean up the air, water, and soil that support us, including such simple yet meaningful tasks as recycling materials and picking up trash along the highways.

5. Working with activity and athletic programs for young people, such as Boy Scouts, Girl Scouts, Little League, and Special Olympics.

6. Supporting and helping in the charitable projects of numerous community, social, and fraternal organizations.

RESPONSIBILITIES AND HEROES

I have spoken about citizenship responsibilities. I close with some observations about the relationship of responsibilities to the matter of heroes. I use the word *heroes* to include both male and female.)

My friend President George Roche of Hillsdale College gives many important insights in his book, *A World without Heroes* (Hillsdale, Michigan: Hillsdale College Press, 1986). Seeking to answer the important question of why our current generation seems to have no heroes, Dr. Roche observes that a hero gains that stature by courageously overcoming significant obstacles to make an extraordinary achievement that is generally recognized as a good thing. He observes that "The hero seeks not happiness but goodness" (Ibid., p. 4).

The kinds of persons who are idolized in our current society, including sports figures and movie or rock stars, are substitutes for heroes, but they are not heroes. The current idols stand for a self-serving pursuit of happiness, not an unselfish sacrifice for goodness. A materialistic or self-serving world cannot produce heroes because such a world has no generally accepted measure to tell us what we should do in the service of others. The genuine hero achieves that status by accomplishments measured against a consensus of what is good and praiseworthy. We cannot have heroes without clear common ideas of what is good or right.

My nominees for heroes are the good mothers and fathers who sacrifice to bear and nurture the leaders of future generations. I wish we had a national consensus on the appropriateness of that characterization, but we live in a time when our national leaders cannot even state a consensus on the definition of *family*.

As I read Dr. Roche's stimulating ideas on heroes, I found myself translating his ideas into the common terms of the law with which I am most familiar. I thought of rights and responsibilities.

As noted earlier, the last half-century of legal and public discourse has concentrated strongly on the language of rights. I suggest that there are few heroes in a world that focuses on rights. Is a person a hero for getting his or her rights? There is justice in that accomplishment, but its only service is self-service. On exceptional occasions some persons can rise to hero status by securing the rights of others, such as the civil rights volunteers of the sixties who put their lives in jeopardy in securing the voting rights of black citizens in the south. But most commonly the gladiators who fight for the rights of others are well paid by legal fees or by public office or prominence. No, the pursuit of rights is rarely the stuff of which heroes are made. And so, in a time of preoccupation with rights, it should not surprise us that we live in a world with few heroes.

Heroes win that status by distinction in the fulfillment of *responsibilities*. If we could resurrect the prominence of responsibilities in our society, we would resurrect the framework of belief and the measures of distinction by which heroes can be recognized and honored.

The citizen responsibilities I have discussed provide such an opportunity. I therefore join my voice to the plea of Dr. George Roche:

> If this tired old planet is to be healed, it will be the old-fashioned way, one by one, with each of us finding the best within us. We all have to be heroes! (Ibid., p. xviii.)

May God bless us in our efforts to fulfill our responsibilities and to rise to the best that is in us.

Let reverence for the laws be breathed by every American mother to the lisping babe that prattles on her lap. Let it be taught in schools, in seminaries, and in colleges. Let it be written in primers, spelling books, and in almanacs. Let it be preached from the pulpit, proclaimed in legislative halls, and enforced in the courts of justice.

—Abraham Lincoln

10

The Integrity of Obeying the Law
PRESIDENT JAMES E. FAUST

I am pleased and honored to be with all of you this evening. My responsibility to you is increased because I realize that all of you could be doing something more enjoyable than listening to me. I wish to begin with an expression of appreciation to all, past and present, who have had any part, in any way, in these annual Freedom Festivals.

On this holiday we celebrate, as we have for more than two hundred years, the establishment of a government in a country unlike any other in the history of the world. It has had at its very heart the concept of a government "instituted of God for the benefit of man" (D&C 134:1). The deepest taproots of our nation and state have lain in the very essence of our humanity, our faith in God. This nation as a democracy has as its basic foundation a government of laws and equality of all before the law. Under the Constitution it has the right and the duty to institute laws to protect its citizenry in their inalienable rights, recognizing that, as the Doctrine and Covenants says, "sedition and rebellion are unbecoming every citizen thus protected, and should be punished accordingly" (D&C 134:5). The government has the right and

---

Address given 2 July 1995.

duty to enact laws, within the institutions set up by the Constitution, which are best calculated to secure the public interest while at the same time preserving the individual rights of its citizenry.

There are laws made by men that govern in the affairs of men, and "that which is governed by law is also preserved by law" (D&C 88:34). Then there are also higher and supernal laws which undergird and overarch all other laws, for, as the Lord said, "he that keepeth the laws of God hath no need to break the laws of the land" (D&C 58:21). Section 88 of the Doctrine and Covenants makes reference to celestial laws: "All kingdoms have a law given; . . . And unto every kingdom is given a law; and unto every law there are certain bounds also and conditions" (D&C 88:36, 38).

The most fundamental function of government is that of maintaining peace in the land—everywhere in the land, and for everyone in the land. This is a real issue for our citizenry. This issue, which has existed from the beginning of our republic, is whether or not we are going to have a peaceful society.

I have lived under military dictatorships for some years of my life. I have a great love for those countries and their people. But in those countries the principal authority is the man who has the rubber stamp that grants authority and rights. The law is, in large measure, what the man in authority decides it is. The system of law in those countries evolved from the Roman system, under which the emperor was above the law and the state was the source of all individual rights. In some of those countries, inadequate respect was shown for stop signs or traffic lights or even civil authority. These countries were controlled in large measure by bureaucracy.

From my experience there I have learned that obedience to law ought to be a matter of one's heart and conscience, reinforced by a patriotic feeling of duty and citizenship. "No man is above the law and no man below it," as Theodore Roosevelt put it. "Nor do we ask any man's permission when we require him to obey it." (Noel F. Busch, *The Story of Theodore Roosevelt and His Influence on Our Times* [New York: Reynal & Company Inc., 1963], p. 305.)

In America we inherited a system of law from England, where even the king was subject to the law. In my lifetime I have seen a decay in the respect for the legal system under which we live, and a disrespect and mistrust for civil authority. In my childhood all police officers were respected and looked up to as friends and protectors, as were judges and congressmen. In the 1995 bombing explosion in Oklahoma City some of the heroes who risked their lives were the firemen and policemen who worked round the clock trying to save the lives of others. Yet these same heroes are often defamed and slandered in other circumstances.

Cynicism and distrust of government are abroad in the land. A growing group of our citizenry, including businessmen and professional people, choose not to obey laws they do not like or think are wrong. Like Mr. Bumble in Dickens's *Oliver Twist*, they challenge what they don't like, as he did when he said, "If the law supposes that, the law is a ass—a idiot" (*Oliver Twist*, chapter 51). I am quick to admit that some laws seem irrational, but they are the law and if wrong should be changed by orderly process. I again draw from Theodore Roosevelt: "The best way to get rid of a bad law is to see that it is uniformly enforced" (Busch, *The Story of Theodore Roosevelt and His Influence on Our Times*, p. 305).

At the risk of being subject to some criticism, I suggest that some think Watergate and the Vietnam War had something to do with this growing cynicism. The Watergate scandal showed the betrayal of trust by those in the highest positions of the Executive Branch. To me, the most remarkable experience of Watergate was that the constitutional processes of government functioned to remove the head of state peacefully from office. We should marvel at the orderly transfer of power of government without bloodshed and without damage to the constitutional institutions of our nation. Many, however, see only the failings of some individuals and overlook the strength of our constitutional processes.

One of the highest duties of citizenship is to defend one's country. This is because in wartime, military service often demands the ultimate sacrifice—life itself.

A principal criticism of the Vietnam War is that it was not a popular war. I personally have never known of any *popular* wars.

Earlier wars fought by our country during my lifetime—World War II, Korea, Vietnam—were not popular with the citizen soldiers who endured the misery, the filth, the agony, and the suffering of fighting. These citizen soldiers wanted desperately for the war to end as quickly as possible so they could return to home and family. As Elder Packer emphasized to those who obeyed the law of the land at the time of the Vietnam War: "Though all the issues of the conflict are anything but clear, the matter of citizenship responsibility is perfectly clear. To you who have answered that call, we say serve honorably and well. Keep your faith, your character, your virtue" (Boyd K. Packer, "The Member and the Military," pp. 2, 11).

Because war is so horrible in its consequences, I think it is hard to defend the settlement of disputes through war. I believe that God "holds men accountable for their acts in relation" to the political decisions that bring wars about (see D&C 134:1).

I served for three years in World War II. During most of that time I was married, being separated from my wife for a considerable period. I was drafted, and I served because it was the law of the land. I was no hero, but I believe I did the right thing. If I had to do it over, I would not try to avoid my wartime obligation to my country. As Cardinal Newman said: "There is such a thing as legitimate warfare: war has its laws; there are things which may fairly be done, and things which may not be done" (John Henry, Cardinal Newman, *Apologia pro Vita Sua* [1864], Mr. Kingsley's Method of Disputation). In my opinion, war may be justified when civilization is placed at risk, as when Adolf Hitler sought to rule the world.

My father was drafted in World War I when his wife was expecting a baby. He served as a machine gunner in the 91st Division in some of the heaviest fighting in France. When he died many years later, he still carried shrapnel wounds in his legs. In recent years, while searching for our family history, we have become acquainted with our German relatives, who have lived on the west bank of the Rhine River for centuries. We learned that these relatives served in the German Army in World War I in the same general area on the other side of the front from where my father served. My father was a Christian and they were Christians. During the war they could have been shooting at each other. I do not have the wisdom to sort out the ultimate morality of war, but I do understand the morality of duty to my country. We have found our German relatives to be decent, God-fearing people. My father served in the American Army because it was the law of the land of his citizenship. His German cousins were in the same position, serving in the German Army because it was the law of their land. They had no power in the grand military or political strategies of that war. They were just decent, law-abiding citizens doing their civil duty no matter how personally abhorrent it was to them.

Last year in this same festival Elder Oaks reminded us, "Even an oppressive government is preferable to a state of lawlessness and anarchy in which the only ruling principle is force and every individual has a thousand oppressors" (Dallin H. Oaks, "Some Responsibilities of Citizenship," July 3, 1994, p. 3).

Some may ask, what is anarchy? The word *anarchy* comes from the Greek anarchos, "having no ruler," and in its broader application characterizes a state of lawlessness or political disorder and chaos due to the absence of governmental authority.

Last April I saw this headline in a newspaper: "Latest karaoke club fire kills 51 in northwest China." The article detailed a rash example of civil disobedience. Government officials had ordered the club to shut down the week before because of physical defects, but the club defied the order. Fire broke out and the inadequate exits prevented victims from escaping. In another incident last December a theater fire in Karamay, China, killed 325. A dance hall fire in November killed 288 more people under similar circumstances. All of this because people thumbed their nose at the authority of the government even though the government had only their safety in mind.

I am well aware of the provision in the United States Constitution regarding the right of citizens to bear arms. Amendment II reads: "A well-regulated Militia, being necessary to the security of a free State, the right of the people to keep and bear Arms, shall not be infringed." But I seriously doubt if the framers of the Constitution intended that children would be bringing guns to school. Does the right to bear arms include a citizenry where some are armed with automatic assault weapons, empowering them to take the law into their own hands by overpowering force? Which is worse, someone who refuses to bear arms *for* his country, or someone who bears arms *against* his country?

The United States, along with other nations, was outrged by the Somalian warlords' complete lawlessness, which resulted in acute hunger, terrible suffering, and vicious abuse of the citizens of Somalia. To restore order, our armed forces were sent into that country with great armed might, with some of our best trained troops and the most sophisticated modern weapons of war. Rival armed militia groups were riding through the streets of Mogadishu and other cities with machine guns mounted on jeeps, terrorizing the people. Our great armed might tried to establish peace by force but were only partially successful for a time. Eventually our soldiers and those of the other nations were obliged to leave the country for their own safety. No central authority could be installed in the country to ensure "domestic tranquility." There is a powerful lesson in this. It is the lesson that government must preserve the peace.

Civil disobedience has become fashionable for a few with strongly held political agendas. Even when causes are meritorious, if civil disobedience were to be practiced by everyone with a cause our democracy would unravel and be destroyed. Civil disobedience is an abuse of political process in a democracy. "No one pretends that democracy is perfect or all-wise," as Winston Churchill once said. "Indeed, it has been said that democracy is the worst form of Government except all those other forms that have been tried from time to time" (*The Oxford Dictionary of Quotations*, Third Edition, [New York: Oxford University Press, 1979], p. 150).

Recently I heard a new convert to our Church urge that the Church resort to civil disobedience and violence because of the moral wrongness of abortion. The position of The Church of Jesus Christ of Latter-day Saints opposing abortion is long-standing and well known. I told him that it was our belief that even though we disagreed with the law, and even though we counselled our people strongly against abortion, and even though we bring into question the membership of those involved in abortion, we are still obliged to recognize the law of the land until it is changed. His response was, "Even if it is wrong?" I tried to explain that when we disagree with a law, rather than resort to civil disobedience or violence we are obliged to exercise our right to seek its repeal or change by peaceful and lawful means.

There is a growing mistrust and distrust for all forms of government and authority. We claim the right to do what we want, but we are often slow to face up to our duty as citizens in a free land. Many of the rising generation have paid little price beyond that of paying taxes for the blessings we enjoy in this country. As some wag has said, the trouble with this generation is that it has not read the minutes of the last session.

An editorial in the *Deseret News* last May pointed up disrespect for the law and our fellow citizens here in the West. The editorial reads:

> A herd of cattle couldn't have ravaged Yuba Reservoir the way a mob of humans did over the holiday weekend. That is significant, considering some have worried that grazing livestock are a threat to Yuba's water quality. Partiers covered the shores and inland camping areas with piles of cans, broken bottles, toilet paper, human waste and mangled lawn furniture. The scene late Monday was a disgraceful testament to a diminished respect in society.
>
> Respect? It could hardly have been on the minds of any of the 30,000 people who cavorted in and around the reservoir. They didn't respect the natural and manmade beauty of the place. They didn't respect the rights of others, as evidenced by the more than 600 people arrested by a squad of officers led by the Juab County sheriff's office. They certainly didn't respect

the officers, hitting one of them with a beer bottle and assaulting another because he tried to arrest a man who had driven over someone else with a vehicle. Most disturbing of all, they didn't respect the people who use the reservoir.

In this complex industrialized society in which we live, the government seems to limit what we do as individuals in countless ways. No one can deny the bureaucratic insensitivity of layers of governments with rule-making authority who are not directly answerable to the voters. This is often frustrating and vexatious to the citizenry. Governmental regulations sometimes restrict the enjoyment of our property rights without just compensation. But the government must not only deal with our local problems but with many problems that are not only national (like national defense) but also global in nature.

Let us take the pollution of the air and water as an example. Those who have been in the largest cities of the world, particularly those in some of the Third World countries, know how poisoned the atmosphere and water can be. Having lived in such cities, I found that every day I had a struggle to breathe. Upon returning to the United States I was grateful for a government that had adequate laws to protect the water and the air so that I could breathe and drink and remain healthy. We are fortunate to have government and industry working together on these problems. Those who claim their rights are being infringed by government are seldom heard to say, "I have the right to drink contaminated water and breathe poisoned air."

There is also the pollution of the air waves, movie theaters, and the print media. If there is to be any control of these media, it must come from the national government, because, like the air we breathe and the water we drink, this type of pollution crosses state and national boundaries. The fact is that only national governments can deal with global problems.

The Declaration of Independence articulates that all men and women are endowed by their Creator with inalienable rights. These rights are guaranteed by seven fundamental rights set forth in the Bill of Rights:

Freedom of speech
Freedom of religion
Freedom of the press
Freedom of peaceful assembly
Freedom from unreasonable search
Right to have a lawyer
Right to have a trial by jury

It becomes the duty of all of us not only to claim these rights for ourselves but also to honor them and secure them for our fellow countrymen.

However, I believe that most governmental problems can usually be handled best at a level closest to the people. The principal suggestion I have this evening to cure some of the ills and irritations of government is to get personally involved. In a democracy, if we are not involved in our duty as citizens we have the kind of government we deserve. President Rex E. Lee of Brigham Young University quoted the famous statement, "Render therefore unto Caesar the things which be Caesar's, and unto God the things which be God's" (Luke 20:25). President Lee stated that in recent times he has found "two separate freestanding commandments concerning our obligation of service to be 'rendered.'" Said President Lee, "If this be true then the true followers of Christ recognize a duty of service not only to deity but also government." (Rex E. Lee, Brigham Young University, April Commencement, April 27, 1995.)

The First Presidency has said: "Members are encouraged to participate as responsible citizens in supporting measures that strengthen society morally, economically, and culturally. They are urged to be actively engaged in worthy causes to improve their communities and make them more wholesome places in which to live and rear families." (First Presidency letter, October 19, 1994.)

There is a widespread feeling that the honored values of this nation are eroding and must be re-enthroned. When someone in good conscience tries to say this, invariably someone else raises the voice, "Whose values?" My answer to that is, everybody's values: time-honored values such as absolute honesty, complete integrity, decency and civility, marriage, independence, industry, thrift, self-reliance, respect for law and order, and hard work. These are human values.

I do not wish to be a voice of doom. I wish to be a voice of confidence and hope in our country. The United States, with all of its challenges and problems, is still the greatest haven of opportunity in the world. Our government has never been more greatly challenged to defend its borders from people from other countries who wish to live here and enjoy the freedoms and opportunities this country affords. The desirability of this country will persist so long as its citizenry are a God-fearing people with the integrity to obey the law of the land. This includes the laws we do not like as well as the laws we do like.

There are natural safeguards in a God-fearing people that promote respect for law and order, decency, and public civility. That restraining influence is the belief that the citizenry will be accountable to their Creator for their conduct under a high moral law. This respect for and adherence to moral law transcends the constraints of the civil and criminal codes. In a people who are not God-fearing, however, these characteristics are notably absent.

Will public civility be lost under the guise of claiming under Constitutional safeguards the rights to freedom of speech? Will tolerance of other faiths and beliefs continue to be diminished by claiming rights under the establishment and free exercise clauses of the Constitution?

Let us resolve, as did the Psalmist who said:

"So shall I keep thy law continually for ever and ever.

"And I will walk at liberty: for I seek thy precepts.

"I will speak of thy testimonies also before kings, and will not be ashamed.

"And I will delight myself in thy commandments, which I have loved.

"My hands also will I lift up unto thy commandments, which I have loved; and I will meditate in thy statutes." (Psalm 119:44–48.)

Notice that this beautiful Psalm says *I* will face up to my personal and public challenges. *I* have an individual responsibility. Abraham Lincoln said it best for all of us at Gettysburg, collectively and individually:

"From these honored dead we take increased devotion to that cause for which they gave the last full measure of devotion; that we here highly resolve that these dead shall not have died in vain; that this nation, under God, shall have a new birth of freedom. And that government of the people, by the people, for the people, shall not perish from the earth."

As the flag unfurls on July Fourth, and with it a fresh wave of national pride, may God help us to increase our personal and individual devotion to the cause of the great country it represents.

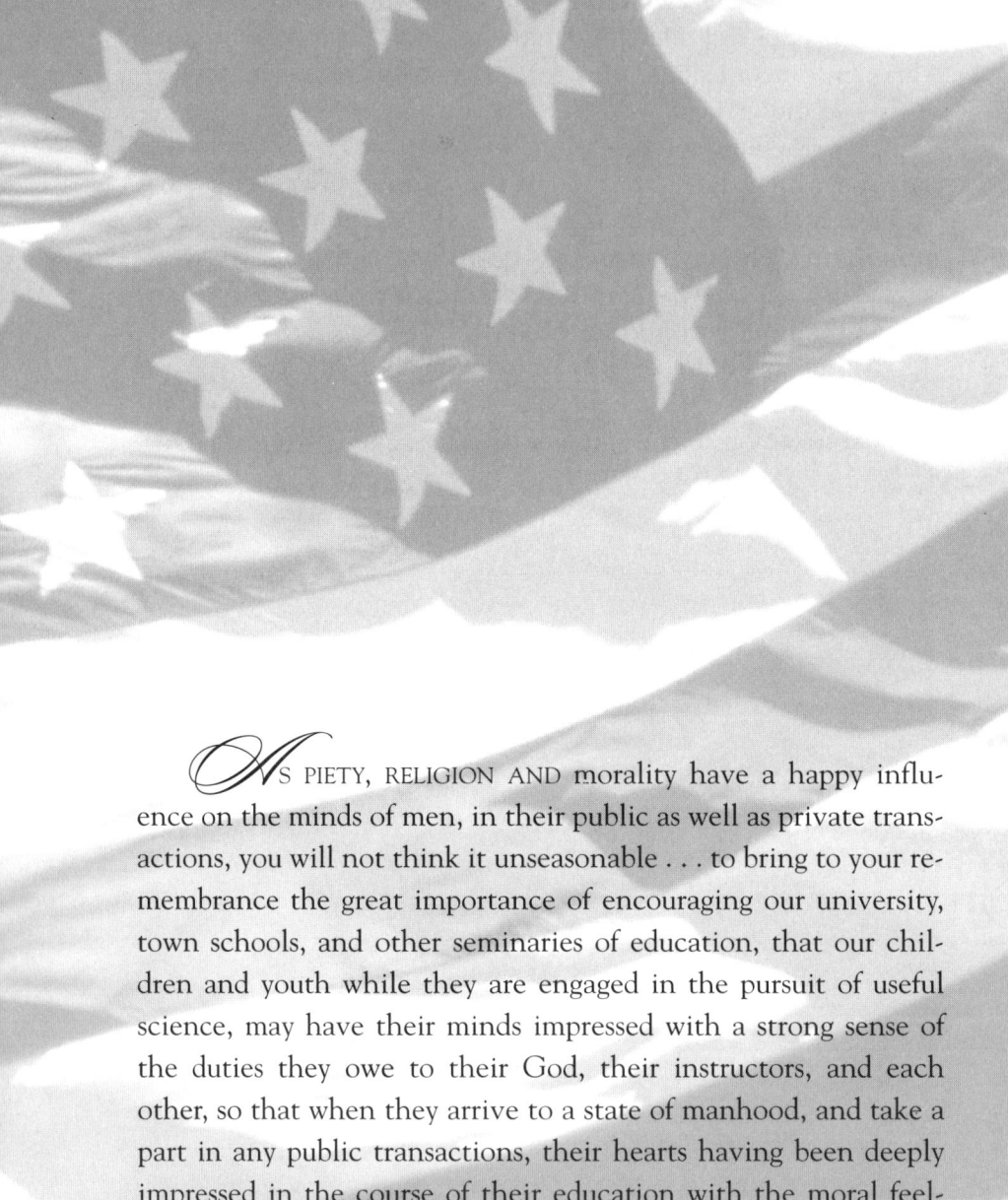

As piety, religion and morality have a happy influence on the minds of men, in their public as well as private transactions, you will not think it unseasonable . . . to bring to your remembrance the great importance of encouraging our university, town schools, and other seminaries of education, that our children and youth while they are engaged in the pursuit of useful science, may have their minds impressed with a strong sense of the duties they owe to their God, their instructors, and each other, so that when they arrive to a state of manhood, and take a part in any public transactions, their hearts having been deeply impressed in the course of their education with the moral feelings—such feelings may continue and have their due weight through the whole of their future lives.

—Samuel Adams

11

"Except the Lord Build the House"
ELDER JEFFREY R. HOLLAND

Dear friends and neighbors, brothers and sisters. Thank you for the invitation to be with you tonight on a campus I dearly love in a community we long called home. I also thank you for the privilege of being involved in what has become a magnificent Fourth of July tradition in this state. I pay tribute to those who do so much to make this annual Freedom Festival all that it has become and all that it will again be this week.

I have loved the Fourth of July for as long as I can remember. In St. George, during my growing-up years virtually every young boy in town slept out of doors on the night of the third of July, carefully positioned in a sleeping bag out on his front lawn. That way he would not miss any of the fireworks and rocketry that my father and other civic leaders helped introduce and perpetuate in what was then a quiet and sleepy southern Utah community.

Actually the front lawn at the Holland home seemed to attract more than its share of boys on the night of the third because on the morning of the Fourth each would find under his pillow a bottle of homemade, hand-bottled, nigh-unto-exploding bottle of root beer they could enjoy at their leisure right at sunrise. That

---
Address given 30 June 1996.

was when the six-piece senior citizen band would ride through town playing with all the zeal (if not quite the precision or tonality) of a John Philip Sousa contingent. Such a patriotic arousal on the morning of the Fourth, followed by Alice Holland's waffles for as many boys as were there to eat them, is one of the sweet and permanent memories of my youth. Thanks again to our Freedom Festival team for providing a younger generation of girls and boys with new memories of what Independence Day in Provo will always mean to them.

Today, however, I have memories of a different kind—and not quite so joyful. They are reflections on my experience of just a few days ago. Last Sunday I addressed the members of The Church of Jesus Christ of Latter-day Saints gathered in Budapest, Hungary, in a large building not far from the beautiful Hungarian Statue of Liberty that overlooks that city, so war-torn and devastated for so much of this century. Just the Tuesday before that I had met with a counterpart group of Latter-day Saints in Prague, the capital of the Czech Republic, a beautiful land that has lived with tyranny and despotism and occupation for nearly three-fourths of this century.

In between those two wonderful experiences in these marvelously renewed nations now bustling with freedom, and loving it, I traveled down between the now-fateful nations of Croatia and Serbia to go into the devastating interior of Bosnia in order to meet with and try to give inspiration to our LDS military troops who are deployed there in a difficult and demanding peacekeeping assignment.

I will leave all the emotion and details of that sobering experience for another day, but suffice it to say I literally wept as I stood on a windswept hill overlooking Sarajevo and saw the scarred remains of what no one would have believed could happen in the enlightened and freedom-granting days of the 1990s. This had been the site of the 1984 Winter Olympics, one of the loveliest little mountain cities in all Europe. And now it appeared like a scene out of the Apocalypse.

These lines from the book of Revelation were riveted in my

mind: "And I looked, and behold a pale horse: and his name that sat on him was Death, and Hell followed with him. And power was given unto them over the fourth part of the earth, to kill with sword, and with hunger, and with death, and with the beasts of the earth."[1] After a very long and demanding trip, with such scenes as those in Bosnia indelibly impressed on my mind and heart forever, I found myself coming home with renewed appreciation for the lines of Henry Van Dyke I had heard in my youth:

So it's home again, and home again, America for me!
My heart is turning home again, and there I long to be
In the land of youth and freedom beyond the ocean bars,
Where the air is full of sunlight and the flag is full of stars.[2]

By and large this is not a time of war for Americans generally, and we feel wonderfully safe in these valleys of the mountains. But I come to you today having just seen war, and war of the worst kind, a kind that can be sobering for us even in the sweet splendor of these summer Utah days. For in this tragedy that was once Yugoslavia I saw *not* the battle lines of large nations or differences that were entire continents apart. No, this was not the stuff of G.I. Joe movies I had seen as a boy in the old Dixie Theater in St. George. What I saw was the tragic, telling, catastrophic effects of a war *between neighbors*, a war between people living on the same street, a war among families clustered in groups of houses exactly like those in which you and I live.

What I saw was not a war of despotism and tyrants—though there have been some of those in this conflict—but it was rather a war of venom and malice and villainy in the human hearts— hatred embedded in human beings who were together very much like you and I live together in Provo and Orem and Pleasant Grove and Santaquin and Payson and anywhere else we might come from tonight. I was brought up short by the stark scenes before me that war is not something always waged by an Adolf Hitler or a Joseph Stalin, those personifications of evil from days of my boyhood. No, in this worst-case example the ruthless and relentless were Adolf who lived across the street and Joseph who owned the home just next door. This tragic Yugoslavian war is horrible most of all because it has been neighbor against neighbor, and although peace has been imposed, fear and disbelief still stare blankly from the faces of the people who have survived that war.

These sobering thoughts about the human heart and the central issue of morality and tolerance and personal character have driven me back on this Fourth of July to a consideration of the foundation of this republic. The reminder that I wish to leave with you tonight is that our special American history and our unique democratic experience in living together and prospering together declares the everlasting truth that freedom and self-government and civility and peace require something from the *people*, not just the government—people who know they must love the noble and demonstrate the moral, people who must reject the darker impulses and influences in this world, people who must practice virtue and protect the high hopes for safety and happiness that they and every one of their neighbors has the right to embrace and uphold. The key to peace and liberty—private or public, individual or national—lies within the hearts and souls of you and me. The hope of "liberty and justice for all" (to quote from our Pledge of Allegiance) is a hope that must emanate from our families, our homes, our schools, and our neighborhoods. The call to patriotism is the call to every one of us, because war of the Bosnian brand is only a neighbor away.

That is a principle upon which this marvelous nation of ours was built. Long before the Declaration of Independence and the Revolution of 1776 a common system of human values had led to that emerging sense of something that was to be called America. Since the first Pilgrims had landed on our eastern shores there had been a belief that these settlers were led by heaven and that they had before them a great mission, an important obligation to live in a certain way and reflect ceratain ideals. They had obligations to God and to their fellow men and women.

In 1620, while still aboard their sailing vessel on their way to

America, our ancestors entered into a covenant known as the Mayflower Compact, in which they stated: "We whose names are underwritten . . . Do by these Presents, solemnly and mutually in the presence of God and one another, covenant and combine ourselves together into a civil Body Politik." One legal scholar reviewing that language termed it a truly "extraordinary statement" with the realization that, in the form of what was virtually a religious covenant, these Pilgrims were voluntarily choosing to limit their personal power and their individual exercise of political force in order to have something larger, something greater, something called the common good.

Some of the clergymen among that band of colonists saw this as a new "promised land" set apart by God for a new people, a new expression of religious living, a new state, even a New Jerusalem. And that would require selfless citizens indeed. As John Winthrop, one of the greatest of all those first Puritans, stated in 1630: "We must consider that we shall be as a City upon a Hill, [where] the eyes of all people are upon us."[3] "We must be knit together in this work as one . . . we must delight in each other, make others' conditions our own, rejoice together, mourn together, labor and suffer together . . . as members of the same body."

A first-generation Puritan layman praised this colonial adventure as the settlement of a new Mount Zion in the American wilderness, and during the Revolution many of the clergy used the pulpit openly and often brazenly for a call to arms, typically referring to the revolutionary troops as the "Armies of Israel." "The finger of God," said Phillip Payson in 1782 "has been so conspicuous in every stage of our glorious struggle, that it seems as if the wonders and miracles performed for Israel of old were repeated over anew for the American Israel in our day."[4]

Many would have agreed with the vision of French philosopher Alexis de Tocqueville, who later visited America in 1831. It seemed to him that this land had been "kept in reserve by the Deity,"[5] that the colonists were "not a mere party of adventurers gone forth to seek their fortune beyond [the] seas, but the germ of a great nation wafted by Providence to a predestined shore[6] . . . I think I see," he wrote, "the destiny of America embodied in the first [believer] who landed on these shores, just as the whole human race was represented by the first man [Adam]."[7]

So our American fathers and mothers believed and lived. As events transpired leading to the Declaration of Independence, the American Revolution, and the adoption of a Constitution, the founders spoke more and more in terms of a "mission" for the new land they occupied, and reference to an intervening Providence appeared increasingly in their writings and their spoken word. Their sense of history and belief in God combined to engender a cautious hypothesis that Providence had placed them in this place and at this time with opportunities that had great import for all humanity for all time to come.

In the Philadelphia Convention, Benjamin Franklin reminded his colleagues that "All of us who were engaged in this struggle must have observed frequent instances of a Superintending providence in our favor. . . . The longer I live," he said, "the more convincing proofs I see of this truth—that God governs in the affairs of men."[8]

James Madison wrote in the *Federalist*, "It is impossible for the man of pious reflection not to perceive in it a finger of that Almighty hand which has been so frequently and signally extended to our relief in the critical stages of the Revolution."[9]

George Washington insisted that the "Supreme Being" had protected "the liberty and happiness of these United States. . . . The hand of Providence has been so conspicuous in all this," he said, "that he must be worse than an infidel that lacks faith, and more than wicked, that has not gratitude enough to acknowledge his obligations [in return]."[10] In his Inaugural Address, Washington stated: "No people can be found to acknowledge and adore the Invisible Hand which conducts the affairs of men more than the people of the United States. Every step by which they have advanced to the character of an independent nation seems to have been distinguished by some token of Providential agency."

And so the theme would continue. In Thomas Jefferson's

Second Inaugural Address, he acknowledged "that Being in whose hands we are, who led our forefathers as Israel of old, from their native land and planted them in a country flowing with all the necessaries and comforts of life, who has covered our infancy with his Providence and our ripe years with his wisdom and power."[11]

The responsibilities of a new nation weighed heavily upon the Founders. Given their understanding of the complexity of man, including the possibility of dark forces and feelings, they were forced to ask themselves: Is a republic even possible? Indeed, were the people of America capable of self-government? Was the "genius of the people" (which meant their total character) strong enough to support any form of democracy?

James Madison spent much of his time attempting to prove that America had been chosen by Providence for this grand experiment in testing the human capacity for self-government. "The free system of government we have established," he said, "[will] produce approbation and a desire for imitation. . . . Our country, if it does justice to itself, will be the workshop of liberty to the Civilized World, and do more than any other for the uncivilized."[12]

The times were such that Thomas Paine wrote in his *Common Sense*, "The cause of America is in great measure the cause of all mankind."[13] John Adams prophesied that if America failed in her divinely appointed mission, it would be "treason against the hopes of the world."[14] And Thomas Jefferson confirmed, "The last hope of human liberty rests on us."[15]

Still, the great question remained: were these American people in this new American nation really capable of fulfilling their personal, ethical, private as well as public responsibilities, especially as they believed them to be God-given responsibilities?

Through their knowledge of history, their commitment to the moral values and traditions in which they believed, and through their own experience, the American founding fathers knew that *a morally corrupt people could never enjoy the luxury of freedom*. Their teacher, the great English philosopher, Edmund Burke, had said it best:

"*Men are qualified for civil liberty in exact proportion to their disposition to put moral chains on their own appetites* [May I repeat that: "Men are qualified for civil liberty in exact proportion to their disposition to put moral chains on their own appetites."] . . . Society cannot exist unless a controlling power upon the will and appetite be placed somewhere, and the less of it there is within, the more there must be without. It is ordained in the eternal constitution of things, that men of intemperate minds cannot be free. Their passions forge their fetters."[16]

Among the most important terms used in this new language of the Republic were "moral sense" and "virtue." Thomas Jefferson, for example, believed that if moral sense and personal virtue had not been God-given within the human being, then the building of any republic—especially the one we enjoy today—would simply have been impossible.

According to Jefferson, "passions and appetites are parts of human nature," but so are "reason and moral sense."[17] "It would have been inconsistent [by God] in [the very act of] creation," he insisted, "to have found man for [life in a] social state, and not to have provided virtue and wisdom enough to manage the concerns of [that] society."[18] "I believe that it is instinct[ive], and innate, that the moral sense is as much a part of our [personal] constitution as that of feeling, seeing, or hearing. A wise Creator must have seen [this as] necessary in [a being] destined to live [together] in society."[19]

But men and women would not always be moral and they would not always demonstrate virtue.

As James Madison wrote in the *Federalist*, "men are not angels," and "good men will not always be at the helm,"[20] therefore "auxiliary precautions" would be necessary: that is, certain checks and balances in government, which would be supportive to a people striving to be virtuous.[21]

But no system of checks and balances can withstand forever the multiplying forces of selfishness, malice, and immorality. The moral sense, though God given, can be damaged and diminished. Virtue, inherent within all, can be compromised and corrupted.

And the founding fathers warned time after time against such a possibility.

George Washington reminded us that "reason and experience both forbid us to expect that national morality can prevail in exclusion of religious principles. It is substantially true, that virtue and morality are a necessary [foundation] of popular government."[22]

At the Constitutional Convention in 1787, Benjamin Franklin voiced his concern that although the new government would likely "be well administered for a course of years," it *could* "end in despotism, as other forms have done before it, when the people have become so corrupted as to need despotic government, being incapable of any other."[23]

John Adams warned two years later: "We have no government . . . capable of contending with human passions unbridled by morality and religion."[24] At another time he wrote, "Liberty can no more exist without virtue . . . than the body can live without a soul."[25] And Samuel Adams added, although "revelation assures us that 'righteousness exalteth a nation,' . . . the public liberty will not long survive the total extinction of morals."[26] "If we are universally vicious and debauched in our manners," he warned, "though the form of our Constitution carries the face of the most exalted freedom, we shall in reality be the most abject of slaves."[27]

In that spirit James Madison cried out: "Is there no virtue among us? If there be not, we are in a wretched situation. No theoretical checks—no form of government—can render us secure. To suppose that any form of government will secure liberty or happiness without any virtue in the people, is a chimerical idea."[28]

With this understanding, a critically important realization came to bear on the minds and hearts of the founding fathers. Success in their endeavors depended not only upon virtue in the people at that time, but it also depended on the continuation of those virtues in every successive generation to come.

Clearly the key to true liberty lay in the human heart, and today that means our hearts—yours and mine and our children and our childrens' children—as well as those of Pilgrims, Puritans, and the original founding fathers.

As Alexander Hamilton said so beautifully: "The sacred rights of mankind are not to be rummaged for among old parchments and musty records. They are written as with a sunbeam in the whole volume of human nature, by the hand of Divinity itself, [upon the soul of man.] . . . The Supreme Being gave existence to man, together with the means of preserving and beautifying that existence. He endowed him with rational faculties, by which he could discern and pursue such things as were consistent with his duty and interest, and invested him with an inviolable right to personal liberty and personal safety."[29]

So America was founded on principles of personal virtue and private morality that would give meaning and vitality to those more technical political principles of constitutional government with its executive, legislative, and judicial branches of activity. Undergirding all of this was the commitment of the individual citizen as well as that of the elected official. From such a personal devotion would come the determination to live together in peace and liberty and safety and freedom. These are blessings we want for ourselves, our children, our neighborhoods, and our world. They are very much the blessings for which this nation was settled and for which that initial War of Independence was fought.

War waged for the triumph of these blessings will still need to be fought in our time, in our day, and forever. We pray it will not be a war of weapons and bullets, but it is a war nonetheless—a daily battle of discipline and hard work and requiring help from heaven. We have to keep winning the peace in every generation by emphasizing over and over the fundamental need for virtue in the human heart. To paraphrase James Madison: "If such concepts as justice, mercy, good faith, integrity, courtesy and all the qualities which elevate the character of a nation and fulfill the ends of government—if these virtues can abide in the hearts of our people and be the objective of our civil establishments, then the cause of freedom and the rights of liberty will acquire a dignity and a luster no despot, tyrant, or warring faction can ever destroy. On the other hand, if families, or communities, or governments should in any way be blotted with the reverse of such cardinal and essential virtues—virtues which have characterized good living and good lives in every age of mankind—if we lose these virtues or pursue the opposite of them, then the great cause that we know as America will be betrayed, dishonored, and finally destroyed." As Mr. Madison said, "If such an immoral and uncivil day should come [to America], then this last and fairest experiment in favor of the rights of man will be turned against him."[30]

Daniel Webster, one of the most distinguished statesmen and political orators of the nineteenth century, said: "Let us not forget the religious character of our origins. Our fathers were brought here by their high veneration for [their faith]. They journeyed by its light, and labored in its hope. They sought to incorporate its principles with the elements of their society, and to diffuse its influence through all their institutions—civil, political and literary. Let us cherish these sentiments, and extend this influence still more widely, in the full conviction that the happiest society [is the one] which partakes in the highest degree of the mild and peaceable spirit of [true Christ-like behavior]."[31]

With my renewed gratitude for the heritage and happiness that has been our history for more than two centuries I say to all, "Except the Lord build the house, they labour in vain that build it."[32] May we live in such a way that the God and Father of us all will continue to bless America, "land that we love." And may He bless all of His children everywhere—especially you and your families—forever. Have a grateful Fourth of July. Thank you and good night.

Notes

1. Revelations 6:8.
2. Cited in *The Home Book of Quotations*, sel. Burton Stevenson (New York: Dodd, Mead & Company, 1934), p. 52.

3. John Winthrop, "A Model of Christian Charity," in Perry Miller and Thomas H. Johnson, *The Puritans* vol. 1 (New York: Harper and Row, 1963), p. 199. See also Sacvan Vercovitch, *The Puritan Origins of the American Self* (New Haven: Yale University Press, 1975.)

4. Cited in James Hitchinson Smylie's "American Clergymen and the Constitution of the United States of America, 1781–1796" (Ph.D. dissertation, Princeton Theological Seminary, Princeton, New Jersey), and quoted in Michael Chadwick, *God's Hand in the Founding of America, As Acknowledged by the Early Clergymen of the United States* (Salt Lake City: Deseret Book Co., 1980), p. 3.

5. Alexis de Tocqueville, *Democracy in America*, trans. Henry Reeve (New York: Knopf, 1945), vol. 1, p. 302.

6. Ibid., p. 34.

7. Ibid., p. 301.

8. Max Farrand, ed., *The Records of the Federal Convention of 1787*, vol. 1, p. 451.

9. *The Federalist*, No. 20.

10. John C. Fitzpatrick, ed., *The Writings of George Washington 1745–1799* (George Washington Bicentennial Commission, 1931; reprinted at Westport, Connecticut, 1970), vol. 12, p. 343.

11. Cited in Richard Vetterli and Gary Bryner, *In Search of the Republic* (Savage, MD: Rowman & Littlefield Publishers, Inc., 1987), p. 68.

12. Adrienne Koch, *Power, Morals, and the Founding Fathers* (Ithaca, N.Y.: Cornell University Press, 1961), p. 105.

13. "There is an exaltation, an excitement, about *Common Sense* that conveys the very uncommon sense of adventure Americans felt as they moved toward independence. With it would come new perils, but also new opportunities, new freedoms. They knew they were on the threshold of a great experience not only for themselves but perhaps for the whole world." Edmund S. Morgan, *The Birth of the Republic* (Chicago: University of Chicago Press, 1956), p. 75.

14. L. H. Butterfield, ed., *Adams Family Correspondence* (Cambridge: Harvard University Press, 1963), pp. 30–31.

15. John Dewey, *The Living Thoughts of Thomas Jefferson* (New York: Longman's, Green, 1940), p. 56.

16. Edmund Burke, *The Works of Edmund Burke*, vol. 4 (Waltham, Mass.: Little, Brown, 1866), pp. 51–52.

17. C. F. Adams, *Writings of John Adams*, vol. 6, p. 115.

18. Lester J. Cappon, ed., *The Adams-Jefferson Letters* (Chapel Hill: University of North Carolina Press, 1959), p. 388.

19. Ibid., p. 492.

20. Willmoore Kendall and George Cary, *The Basic Symbols of the American Political Tradition* (Baton Rouge: Louisiana State University Press, 1970). See also David Epstein, *The Political Theory of the Federalist* (Chicago: University of Chicago Press, 1984).

21. *The Federalist*, No. 51.

22. George de Huszar, et al., *Basic American Documents* (Ames, Iowa: Littlefield, Adams, 1953), vol. 2, pp. 108–9.

23. Max Farrand, ed., *The Records of the Federal Convention of 1787*, vol. 2, pp. 641–42.

24. C. F. Adams, *The Works of John Adams*, vol. 9, p. 229.

25. Bernard Bailyn, "A Fear of Conspiracy against Liberty," in Robert F. Berkhofer, Jr., *The American Revolution* (Boston: Little, Brown, 1971), p. 101.

26. Letter from Samuel Adams to John Scollary of Boston, April 30, 1776; from the *Samuel Adams Papers*, Bancroft Transcripts, New York Public Library.

27. William V. Wells, *The Life and Public Services of Samuel Adams* (Boston: Little, Brown, 1865), vol. 1, p. 22–23.

28. Jonathan Elliot, ed., *The Debates in Several State Conventions on the Adoption of the Federal Constitution* (Philadelphia: Lippincott, 1890), vol. 2, p. 175.

29. Alexander Hamilton, "The Farmer Refuted," (February, 1775); John C. Hamilton, ed., *The Works of Alexander Hamilton*, vol. 2 (New York: Charles S. Francis, 1851), p. 80.

30. Gaillard Hunt, ed., *The Writings of James Madison* (New York: G. P. Putnam, 1902), vol. 1, pp. 459–60.

31. Cited in *The Treasure Chest*, ed. Charles L. Wallis [New York: Harper & Row, Publishers, 1965], p. 177.

32. Psalm 127:1.

America, under the smiles of a Divine Providence, the protection of a good government, and the cultivation of manners, morals, and piety, cannot fail of attaining an uncommon degree of eminence, in literature, commerce, agriculture, improvements at home and respectability abroad.

—George Washington

12

Our Nation's True Source of Strength
PRESIDENT GORDON B. HINCKLEY

It is wonderful to be with you as we celebrate Freedom. Human liberty is such a precious and remarkable thing that it is worthy of a great festival.

We have heard this remarkable choir. They sing with such tremendous power. This choir has become a great national treasure. Its roots reach back to the pioneer beginnings of these mountain communities. We have had a wonderful time listening to them. We might wish that they could go on all evening. At the conclusion of my remarks they will sing the *Battle Hymn of the Republic*, which has stirred audiences throughout the world.

"Mine eyes have seen the glory of the coming of the Lord;
He is trampling out the vintage where the grapes of wrath
    are stored.
He hath loosed the fateful lightning of his terrible, swift sword;
His truth is marching on.
He has sounded forth the trumpet that shall never call retreat;
He is sifting out the hearts of men before his judgment seat.
Oh, be swift, my soul, to answer him; be jubilant my feet!

Address given 29 June 1997.

Our God is marching on.
In the beauty of the lilies, Christ was born across the sea,
With a glory in his bosom that transfigures you and me.
As he died to make men holy, let us live to make men free,
While God is marching on." (*Hymns* no. 60)

This great hymn of hope stirs us now as it did more than a century ago when it was first sung.

I promise you, every one of you, that you will be moved in your hearts as you again hear these talented voices singing out those marvelous and eloquent words.

These words speak of the theme of this meeting. That theme is recognition of and trust in the Almighty, who has guided this nation since its inception. I salute Crystal Jolley for the excellent talk she has given.

A news magazine writer asked me the other day during an interview concerning my belief in the Constitution. I replied that I felt it was inspired, that both the Declaration of Independence and the Constitution of the United States were brought forth under the inspiration of God to establish and sustain the freedom of the people of this nation.

I told him that I looked upon the founding fathers as men who believed in God, as men who prayed to God, as men who recognized God and wished to do His will.

What a singular and remarkable group they were! As I look across the world today I search in vain for such a group as walked together across the stage of history when this nation was born.

Charles Malik, secretary general of the United Nations, once said on this campus:

> I respect all men, and it is from disrespect for none that I say there are no great leaders in the world today. In fact, greatness itself is laughed to scorn. You should not be great today—you should sink yourself into the herd, you should not be distinguished from the crowd, you should simply be one of the many.
>
> The commanding voice is lacking. The voice which speaks little, but which when it speaks, speaks with compelling moral

authority—this kind of voice is not congenial to this age. The age flattens and levels down every distinction into drab uniformity. Respect for the high, the noble, the great, the rare, the specimen that appears once every hundred or every thousand years, is gone. Respect at all is gone! If you ask whom and what people do respect, the answer is literally nobody and nothing. This is simply an unrespecting age—it is the age of utter mediocrity. To become a leader today, even a mediocre leader, is a most uphill struggle. You are constantly and in every way and from every side pulled down. One wonders who of those living today will be remembered a thousand years from now—the way we remember with such profound respect Plato, and Aristotle, and Christ, and Paul, and Augustine, and Aquinas.

If you believe in prayer, my friends, and I know you do, then pray that God send great leaders, especially great leaders of the spirit. (Excerpted from a speech by Charles H. Malik, printed in *BYU Studies*, vol. 16, no. 4, pp. 541–51.)

Just think for a moment of George Washington, of Franklin, of Madison, of the Adamses, of Patrick Henry, Thomas Jefferson, and their associates who signed the Declaration of Independence or participated in the Constitutional Convention. Where in all the world today can even one or two such men be found, let alone the great aggregation who participated in the birth of America?

Can anyone deny that they were raised up unto this very purpose, that working together they brought forth on this continent an independent nation, at the risk of their lives, their fortunes, and their sacred honor?

It is my conviction that while we have had a few great leaders since then, there has not been before or since so large a group of talented, able, and dedicated men as those whom we call the founding fathers of our nation.

For as long as they lived, they acknowledged the hand of the Almighty in the affairs of this republic.

We have on our coinage and our currency a national motto. It simply says, "In God We Trust."

I know of no other nation with such a motto. Other nations use the phrase, "By the grace of God." But none other categorically states, "In God We Trust."

I believe that this is the foundation upon which this nation was established, an unequivocal trust in the power of the Almighty to guide and defend us.

The hand of the Almighty was manifest when the United States of America came into being. It was evident even before then. Before disembarking from the *Mayflower* our Pilgrim fathers drafted and signed the compact which was to become the instrument of their governance, the first such document drafted on this continent. It began with these words: "In the name of God, amen." It went on to say that the signers "by these presents solemnly and mutually in the presence of God, and one another, covenant and combine ourselves together into a civil body politic." (*Harvard Classics*, vol. 43, p. 62).

When George Washington resigned his commission as general of the army, he wrote, "I consider it an indispensable duty to close this last act of my Official life, but commending the interests of our dearest Country to the protection of Almighty God, and those who have the superintendence of them, to His holy keeping" (*George Washington, A Collection*, p. 273).

As we have been reminded, in his first inaugural address in 1789 he stated, "No people can be bound to acknowledge and adore the invisible hand, which conducts the affairs of men, more than the people of the United States. Every step, by which they have advanced to the character of an independent nation, seems to have been distinguished by some token of providential agency." (*Harvard Classics*, vol. 43, p. 242).

We posted the colors tonight and stood and gave the Pledge of Allegiance to the flag of the United States and "to the Republic for which it stands." We said, "One nation, under God, indivisible, with liberty and justice for all." That phrase, "One nation, under God," essentially comes from Abraham Lincoln. In the great Gettysburg Address he stated "that this nation, under God, shall have a new birth of freedom."

That phrase was not in the Pledge of Allegiance that was spoken when I was a boy. Back in those days all of us in grade school, when the weather permitted, would form at the front steps of the school. The flag would be posted and we would recite together the Pledge of Allegiance before going into the building for our daily school work.

I am grateful that the words "One nation, under God" have been added to our pledge. To me it is tremendously meaningful. There are those in this nation today who would delete all of this reference to Deity. They would take it out of the Pledge of Allegiance, they would take it from our coinage, they would remove it from any mention in our national life.

When Margaret Thatcher was on this campus and I was talking with her she said: "I cannot understand it. You have the motto 'In God We Trust' on your coinage. And yet you cannot mention the name of Deity in the classrooms of your schools." She wondered, and I wonder, about our consistency.

At this meeting tonight the first verse of our national anthem was sung. We seldom hear the third verse, which includes these words:

Oh, thus be it ever, when free men shall stand
Between their loved homes and the war's desolation!
Blest with vict'ry and peace, may the heav'n rescued land
Praise the Pow'r that hath made and preserved us a nation!
Then conquer we must, when our cause it is just,
And this be our motto: "In God is our trust!" (*Hymns* no. 340).

As boys who would grow to become citizens of this nation, we repeated the Scout Oath, including these words: "On my honor, I will do my best, to do my duty to God, and my country." Now even that is being challenged in the courts of the land.

According to the *Wall Street Journal* the state of New Jersey last year passed a law banishing the mention of God from state courtroom oaths. Following this action by the legislature, a country judge decided to ban Bibles for such oaths because "you-know-who is mentioned inside." (*Wall Street Journal*, July 31, 1996.)

Without acknowledgment of Deity, without recognition of the Almighty as the ruling power of the universe, the all-important element of personal and national accountability shrinks and dies. Are we so arrogant as to believe that we can get along without Him? We see the manifestation of that arrogance in the great host of social problems with which we deal these days. Teen pregnancy, abandoned families, failure to recognize the property and rights of others, gangs of young people cruising the streets of our cities, and many other problems like these have resulted, in substantial part at least, from failure to recognize there is a God to whom someday each of us must give an accounting. The wars in which this nation has been involved during this the most bloody of all centuries have resulted from the greed, the avarice, the arrogance, the conceit and egotism of men in power who sought to enslave and exercise dominion over others. Their very attitude has been totally incompatible with recognition of an Almighty to whom each of us is accountable. There can be no doubt of the sickness in our society today. We cannot build prisons fast enough to accommodate the need. Humanism has replaced worship in the lives of so very many. We are forsaking the Almighty, and I fear He is forsaking us. We are closing the door against the God whose sons and daughters we are. We sing "My country, 'tis of thee, Sweet land of liberty." We need to sing again and again the fourth verse of that hymn:

> Our fathers' God, to thee
> Author of liberty,
> To thee we sing;
> Long may our land be bright
> With freedom's holy light.
> Protect us by thy might,
> Great God, our King! (*Hymns* no. 339).

Going back to George Washington's first inaugural speech, he voiced the hope "that the foundations of our national policy will be laid in the pure and immutable principles of private morality."

He went on to say, "There is no truth more thoroughly established, than that there exists . . . an indissoluble union between virtue and happiness, between duty and advantage, between the genuine maxims of an honest and magnanimous policy, and the solid rewards of public prosperity and felicity; since we ought to be no less persuaded that the propitious smiles of heaven can never be expected on a nation that disregards the eternal rules of order and right, which heaven itself has ordained" (Op. cit., p. 243). The psalmist of old wrote, "The counsel of the Lord standeth forever, . . . blessed is the nation whose God is the Lord" (Psalm 33:11–12).

Paul the Apostle declared: "Where the Spirit of the Lord is, there is liberty" (2 Corinthians 3:17).

I believe we are paying a very high price for our growing secularism. Jefferson said: "God, who gave us life, gave us liberty. Can the liberties of a nation be secure when we have removed a conviction that these liberties are a gift of God?" (*In Love With Eloquence*, p. 30). Lincoln declared, "What constitutes the bulwark of our own liberty and independence? It is not our frowning battlements, our bristling seacoasts . . . our reliance is in the love of liberty which God has planted in us. Our defense is in the spirit which prized liberty as the heritage of all men, in all lands everywhere" (Ibid., p. 33).

I am convinced that if we are to continue to have the freedoms which came of the inspiration of the Almighty to our founding fathers, we must return to the god who is their true Author. We need to worship Him in spirit and in truth. We need to acknowledge His all-powerful hand. We need to humble ourselves before Him and seek His guidance in all that concerns matters of state. Do we believe in the separation of church and state? Of course, we do. But that belief does not preclude a constant petition to the Almighty for wisdom and guidance as we walk through these perilous times.

We celebrate the freedom of our nation. We hold this festival in remembrance of this greatest of all boons and blessings. May we look to Him as the Author of our liberty. Is it too much to expect that prayer, public and private, be once again established in our national and private lives? Then, with a general acknowledgment of the God in whom we put our trust, we may expect a diminution in our social problems, an increase in public and private morality, and a renewed sense of freedom and liberty.

I realize that after the choir sings we shall have a benediction on this sacred service. But if you will bear with me I wish to conclude my remarks with a few words of solemn prayer. I invite all to lower your heads and close your eyes.

O God, our Eternal Father, Thou who presides over the nations and their people, we come unto Thee in prayer. We thank Thee for this great and sovereign nation of which we are citizens. Touch the minds of those of our Congress that they shall stand tall and independent in defense of the liberty of the people. Bless the Chief Executive. He is our president. Let Thy Spirit move upon him to bring to pass those measures which will lift the burdens of government from the backs of the people and keep this nation, under God, a citadel of freedom standing as an example to all the world. Bless the Supreme Court of the United States, which in recent days has declared unconstitutional a measure designed to secure the religious liberty of the people of this nation. May a way be found under Thy divine inspiration to bring to pass another measure which will be sustained by the Court.

May Thy peace rest upon this nation. May we as a people look to Thee and live. May the benevolent hand of the Almighty protect us from the evil forces of the world. May humanism and secularism bend to an increased acknowledgment of Thee as our Father and our God.

May a spirit of brotherhood spread throughout the land.

As we pray to Thee we do so in our manner, and respect the prayers of others who speak after their manner, that Thou will hear us all as we lift our voices in behalf of our nation. Almighty Father, hear us, guide us, protect us. Make us both strong and benevolent before the world. Forgive our erring ways. May we turn back to Thee in our search for wisdom, for guidance, for direction, we humbly ask in the name of Jesus Christ, amen.

Index

— A —

Adams, John, on Constitution needing moral and religious people, 97
 on Declaration of Independence, 3, 81
 on hopes of the world, 143
 on morality and religion as principles of freedom, 80
 on morality and religion in government, 84
 on need for moral and religious citizens, 24
 on need for morality and religion, 145
 on settlement of America as design of Providence, 56
 on virtue being required for liberty, 145
Adams, John Quincy, on America offering freedom, 64
Adams, Samuel, on freedom requiring virtue, 90
 on learning duties to God, 136
 on liberty requiring morality, 145
Agency, and accountability, 67
 requires freedom and responsibility, 21
America, as workshop of liberty, 143, 147
 brings hope to world, 97, 143
 challenges in, 32–36
 divine destiny of, 150
 guided by God, 3, 141–42, 154–55
 offers freedom, 64
 spiritual foundations of, 1–7
 virtues of, 30–32
Authority, of government, 129–31
 respecting, 104

— B —

Bates, Katherine Lee, on liberty in law, 66
Benson, Ezra Taft, on divine origin of rights given in Bill of Rights, 19
 on people being superior to government, 21
Bill of Rights, controversy over, 70–71
 divine inspiration of, 18–19
Bowen, Catherine Drinker, on miracle of Constitutional Convention, 99
Burke, Edmund, on civil liberty requiring moral chains on appetites, 143–44
 on good men doing nothing, 8

— C —

Chesterton, G. K., on creating nation with a soul, 84
Churchill, Winston, on democratic form of government, 60, 130

Citizenship, avoiding responsibilities of, 105–7, 110–15
developing, 8–9, 53–54
responsibilities of, 23–25, 105–7
Civil disobedience, 130–31
Clark, J. Reuben, on allegiance to Constitution, 23
on Constitution growing to meet needs, 17
on Constitution as part of his religion, 17
on constitutional protection of minorities, 22–23
on union in branches of government, 18
Common good, aim of Pilgrims, 141
Communism, collapse of, 60
Community involvement, importance of, 8–9
"The Concord Hymn" (poem), 40–41
Constitution (U.S.), allegiance to, 23
as model for other constitutions, 71
divinely inspired, 5, 11–26, 82–83, 152
fulfilled promise of liberty, 70
fundamental principles of, 17–23
grows to meet needs, 17
merit of, 10, 71
miracle of, 12, 99
need to study, 8, 24
ratification of, 15–16, 100–101
will hang by a thread, 54
Constitutional Convention, history of, 4–5
described, 13–15
Curtis, George William, on minuteman, 41

— D —

Debt, America's 94
Declaration of Independence, brought change in principle, 70
celebrating, 81
divinely inspired, 3, 152
doctrine of, 2–3
Deficit, need to decrease, 116
Democracy, full meaning of, 59
merit of, 60, 95, 130
requires virtuous people, 145
Discipline, required for discipleship, 66
stem of freedom, 62
Division of powers, as inspired principle of Constitution, 19–20
Drake, Joseph Rodman, on flag, 51
Drugs, lessen personal freedom, 61–62
problem of, 50, 96

— E —

Education, regarding citizenship, 8
spiritual, 62–63
Emerson, Ralph Waldo, on battle for freedom, 40–41
Equal Rights Amendment, and possible effect on constitutional rights, 20
Equality, before law, 22

— F —

Faith, as root of nation, 125
important to nation, 1–2, 9
required for full freedom, 66
Family, and strength of democracy, 54–55

as foundation of society, 7
educating, 8
important to society, 36
responsibility for, 54
rights of, 20
Fathers, to be spiritual leaders in families, 7–8
First Amendment, interpretations of, 83–91
Flag, 51
Flexner, James Thomas, on George Washington, 100
Founders, and sense of destiny, 142–47
 greatness of, 99, 152, 153
 led by God, 142–43
 spirituality of, 3–6
Francisco, Peter, hero of American Revolution, 42–43
Franklin, Benjamin, on acceptance of Constitution, 16, 120
 on concern that people might become corrupted, 145
 on God governing affairs of men, 4–5, 142
 on merit of Constitution, 10
Freedom, comes from God, 7, 157
 founded on morality and religion, 24, 80, 84, 115, 145
 meaning of, 58–59
 price of, 6
 requires chaining appetites, 143–44
 requires discipline, 62
 requires efforts of people, 142
 requires morality, 145
 requires participation, 115
 requires restraints, 38
 requires vigilance, 62
 requires virtues, 90, 145, 146–47
 to worship God, 1–2

— G —

Gladstone, William, on U.S. Constitution, 71
God, as author of liberty, 24, 67
 as source of freedoms and blessings, 7
 central to America's destiny, 141–43, 151–58
 forgetting, 33
 governs affairs of men, 4–5, 142
 gratitude to, x
 guidance of, 154
 imitating characteristics of, 28
 importance to nation, 1–5, 9
 inspires work on U.S. Constitution, 5, 11–26, 82–83, 152
 looking to, 34–37
 protection of, 142, 154
 trust in, 155
Government, and taxes, 110–12
 authority of, 112–15
 democratic form of, 60, 95, 130
 Latter-day Saints required to uphold, 107–9
 principles of, 92
Gratitude, for blessings to America, x, 24
Great Compromise, 15

— H —

Hamilton, Alexander, and Bill of Rights, 70–71
 and Constitution, 13
 on God-given rights and responsibilities, 146
Havel, Vaclav, on bi-polar view of world, 60
 on full sense of democracy, 59
Hendee, Hannah, heroine of American Revolution, 43–46

Henry, Patrick, on Washington's sound judgment, 77
Heritage, includes Christian religion, 36
Heroes, fulfill responsibilities, 122–23
Hinckley, Gordon B., prays for nation, 158
Hope, America's, 97, 143
    sharing example of, 66

— J —

Jefferson, Thomas, and support of Constitution, 16
    foresees problems of big cities, 96
    on America as last hope of human liberty, 143
    on gifts of God, 157
    on God leading forefathers, 142–43
    on greatness of George Washington, 68
    on need for reason and moral sense, 144
    on price of freedom, 6

— K —

Knowledge, need to share, 62–67

— L —

Lamm, Richard, handicaps of American system, 33–34
Law, rule of, 23, 57–58, 65, 125–27
Leaders, early American, 71–79
Leadership, impact of righteous, 71, 78–79
Lee, Rex E., on duty of service, 133
    on interplay of freedoms, 99

Liberty. See Freedom
Light of Christ, binds human family together, 53
Lincoln, Abraham, on danger of forgetting God, 90–91
    on dependence on power of God, 7
    on government by the people, 14, 135
    on hope of liberty for all people, 97
    on liberty being given by God, 157
    on nation being on Lord's side, 83
    on nation under God, 154–55
    on reverence for laws, 124
Lowell, James Russell, on British in America, 39

— M —

MacArthur, Douglas, on sound of battlefield, 94
Madison, James, and Constitution, 13
    on America as experiment in favor of rights of man, 147
    on America as workshop of liberty, 143
    on checks and balances, 144
    on delegates to Constitutional Convention, 15
    on divinity in work on U.S. Constitution, 5
    on finger of Almighty in Revolution, 142
    on governing ourselves according to Ten Commandments, 83
    on government requiring virtue of people, 145
    on self-government, 24

Index

Magna Charta, written guarantee of rights, 19
Malik, Charles, on need for respect, 153
Mason, George, on adherence to fundamental principles, 92
Maxwell, Neal A., on obedience to the unenforceable, 106
Mayflower Compact, forms union under God, 154
Military service, patriotism of, 93–94
  U.S. citizens' responsibility for, 109–10
Mill, John Stuart, on exertion necessary for preserving free government, 98
Minorities, rights of, 22
Morality, and freedom, 53
  at foundation of government, 140
  as foundation of national policy, 101–2
  essential to preserve freedom, 48
  necessary to American government, 24
  necessary to liberty, 144–46
  need for, 62
Mother, protects children, 43–46
"My Country, 'Tis of Thee" (song), 24, 67

— N —

Newman, Cardinal, on legitimate warfare, 128

— O —

Oaks, Dallin, on anarchy, 129
Obedience, essential to liberty, 66
  to the unenforceable, 95, 106

— P —

Packer, Boyd K., on citizenship responsibility, 128
Paine, Thomas, on cause of America as cause of mankind, 143
Participation, in government, 133
  required for perpetuation of freedom, 115
Patriotism, as steady dedication, 25
  meanings of, 93–95
Payson, Phillip, on God helping in struggle to build America, 141
People, as source of governmental power, 14, 20–21
  may become too corrupted to govern, 145
Pilgrims, combine into body politic, 140–41, 154
  spiritual motives of, 1–2
Pinckney, Charles, on divinity in work on U.S. Constitution, 5
Plymouth Colony, founded on faith, 1–2
Popular sovereignty, as inspired principle of Constitution, 20–23
Pornography, lessens personal freedom, 61
  easy distribution of, 87
  problems of, 96
Power, balances of, 116–17
  limits on federal, 117–18
Prayer, important to George Washington, 75, 77
  in public meetings, 86
  need for, 50
  for nation, 158
Preparation, so that God will intervene in our behalf, 7–9

— R —

Regulations, benefits and restrictions of, 132–33
Religion, free exercise of, 35, 83–91
  hostility to, 67, 86–88
  in Bill of Rights, 35
  in politics, 34, 101
Respect, lack of, 131–32
  need for, 153
Responsibilities, avoiding, 105–7, 110–15
  of citizens, 23–25, 105–7, 128–29, 133–34
  fulfilled by heroes, 122–23
Responsibility, individual, 35–36
  necessary to maintain freedoms, 21–22
  root of freedom, 62
Righteousness, and the nation, 1, 36–37
Rights, of majority and of individual, 50–52
Roche, George, on finding the best within us, 123
  on heroes seeking goodness, 122
Rogers, Will, on government and taxes, 110
Roosevelt, Theodore, on getting rid of bad law, 127
  on rule of law, 126

— S —

Scout Oath, acknowledges God, 155
Self-control, importance of, 95–99
Self-government, requires exertion, 98
  requires virtuous people, 145
  See also Democracy; Government
Separation of powers, as inspired principle of Constitution, 18
Service, as duty, 133
  See also Military service; Participation
Single-interest groups, cautions concerning, 119–21
Smith, Joseph, on Constitution not being broad enough, 17
Smith, Joseph F., on America bringing freedom to those in bondage, 64
Smith, Samuel F., on God as author of liberty, 24, 67
Sobran, M. J., on religious conviction, 87
Sovereignty, of people, 113–15
State sovereignty, importance of, 12–13
Stevenson, Adlai, on patriotism, 25
Strength, from the ordinary family, 54
  of America, 32–33, 35
  moral, 48

— T —

Taxes, U.S. citizens' responsibility for, 110–12
Technology, sharing, 65
Thatcher, Margaret, on individual responsibility, 35–36
  on trusting God, 155
Tocqueville, Alexis de, on aloneness in democracy, 95
  on America's greatness and goodness, 32
  on guidance of Providence, 141–42
Tolkien, J.R.R., on looking out for future generations, 95
Tuchman, Barbara, on America's founding fathers, 99

— U —

Union, as purpose of Constitution, 13

as purpose of Pilgrims, 141, 154
Urban decay, 96

— V —

Values, in modern society, 89–91
Van Dyke, Henry, on America as home, 30, 139
Vigilance, and happiness, 101, 156–57
  flower of freedom, 62
  foundation of popular government, 145
Volunteering, and participatory citizenship, 121

— W —

War, and consequences, 127–29
  between neighbors, 139–40
  horrors of, 47–49, 69
  without claiming territory, 31
Washington, George, and Constitutional Convention, 13
  and prayer, 75, 77
  and wise use of power, 100
  described, 72–77
  greatness of, 68
  on America's divine destiny, 150
  on connection between virtue and happiness, 101, 156–57
  on divine intervention in American success, 3
  on God conducting affairs of nation, 142
  on gratitude to God, x
  on guidance of God, 154
  on imitating God's characteristics, 28
  on liberty of conscience, 90
  on miracle of creation of Constitution, 12
  on need for religious principle, 83
  on protection of God, 154
  on religion and morality in politics, 34, 101
  on religious rights, 86
  on respecting authority of government, 104
  on Supreme Being protecting liberty, 142
  on virtue and morality as foundation of popular government, 145
  protected by God, 74–75, 76–77
Webster, Daniel, on connection between liberty and restraint, 38
  on John Adams and Declaration of Independence, 3
  on religious character of America's origins, 147
Wells, Kenneth D., on need for responsible personal conduct, 106
Wildavsky, Aaron, on interaction of people and leaders, 98–99
Williams, Roger, and religious freedom, 85–86
Wilson, James, attacked by mob, 100
  looks beyond own time, 93
Winthrop, John, on being knit together, 141
Woman, strength of, 43–46
Woodruff, Wilford, on God-given law and agency, 67
  on spirituality of founding fathers, 6
Worship, freedom of, 35

— Y —

Young, Brigham, on being prepared, 6–7

America's Freedom Festival at Provo is an independent, nondenominational, nonpolitical organization that produces an expansive, exciting annual celebration held to commemorate America's numerous freedoms. The festival's mission is:

> To celebrate and rejoice in the founding of the United States of America; to instill gratitude and appreciation of freedom and the love of country; to remind everyone within the reach of the festival of our privileges and responsibilities as citizens of the United States of America.

With more than eighty years of tradition and roughly thirty different events spanning four weeks in June and July, America's Freedom Festival at Provo is one of the largest annual Independence Day celebrations in America. It is centered in traditional family-oriented values. As a not-for-profit foundation, the festival is overseen by a board of trustees and executive committee and is assisted by literally thousands of volunteers locally, regionally, and nationally who make this annual patriotic celebration possible.

For more information, write to the festival or visit its Web site:

America's Freedom Festival at Provo
P.O. Box 2230
Provo, UT 84603
www.freedomfestival.org